AS OF 1/1/2016
Acushnet Public Library
232 Middle Rd
Acushnet, MA 02743

 **W9-BYH-921**

INTRODUCING
ISSUES WITH
OPPOSING
VIEWPOINTS®

Cosmetic Surgery

H.G. Robert, *Book Editor*

GREENHAVEN PRESS
A part of Gale, Cengage Learning

GALE
CENGAGE Learning®

Farmington Hills, Mich • San Francisco • New York • Waterville, Maine
Meriden, Conn • Mason, Ohio • Chicago

Russell Memorial Library
88 Main Street
Acushnet, MA 02743

Patricia Coryell, *Vice President & Publisher, New Products & GVRL*
Douglas Dentino, *Manager, New Products*
Judy Galens, *Acquisitions Editor*

© 2015 Greenhaven Press, a part of Gale, Cengage Learning

WCN: 01-100-101

Gale and Greenhaven Press are registered trademarks used herein under license.

For more information, contact:
Greenhaven Press
27500 Drake Rd.
Farmington Hills, MI 48331-3535
Or you can visit our Internet site at gale.cengage.com

ALL RIGHTS RESERVED.
No part of this work covered by the copyright herein may be reproduced, transmitted, stored, or used in any form or by any means graphic, electronic, or mechanical, including but not limited to photocopying, recording, scanning, digitizing, taping, Web distribution, information networks, or information storage and retrieval systems, except as permitted under Section 107 or 108 of the 1976 United States Copyright Act, without the prior written permission of the publisher.

For product information and technology assistance, contact us at

Gale Customer Support, 1-800-877-4253
For permission to use material from this text or product, submit all requests online at
www.cengage.com/permissions

Further permissions questions can be e-mailed to permissionrequest@cengage.com

Articles in Greenhaven Press anthologies are often edited for length to meet page requirements. In addition, original titles of these works are changed to clearly present the main thesis and to explicitly indicate the author's opinion. Every effort is made to ensure that Greenhaven Press accurately reflects the original intent of the authors. Every effort has been made to trace the owners of copyrighted material.

Cover image © sheff/Shutterstock.com

LIBRARY OF CONGRESS CATALOGING-IN-PUBLICATION DATA

Cosmetic surgery / H.G. Robert, book editor.
   pages cm.—(Introducing issues with opposing viewpoints)
 Summary: "Introducing Issues with Opposing Viewpoints: Cosmetic Surgery: Introducing Issues with Opposing Viewpoints is a series that examines current issues from different viewpoints, set up in a pro/con format"—Provided by publisher.
  Includes bibliographical references and index.
  ISBN 978-0-7377-7233-3 (hardback)
 1. Surgery, Plastic—Social aspects. I. Robert, H. G.
  RD119.C6813 2015
  617.9'52—dc23
                            2014030231

Printed in the United States of America
1 2 3 4 5 6 7 19 18 17 16 15

Contents

Chapter 3: Is Cosmetic Surgery for Everyone?

Foreword

Indulging in a wide spectrum of ideas, beliefs, and perspectives is a critical cornerstone of democracy. After all, it is often debates over differences of opinion, such as whether to legalize abortion, how to treat prisoners, or when to enact the death penalty, that shape our society and drive it forward. Such diversity of thought is frequently regarded as the hallmark of a healthy and civilized culture. As the Reverend Clifford Schutjer of the First Congregational Church in Mansfield, Ohio, declared in a 2001 sermon, "Surrounding oneself with only like-minded people, restricting what we listen to or read only to what we find agreeable is irresponsible. Refusing to entertain doubts once we make up our minds is a subtle but deadly form of arrogance." With this advice in mind, Introducing Issues with Opposing Viewpoints books aim to open readers' minds to the critically divergent views that comprise our world's most important debates.

Introducing Issues with Opposing Viewpoints simplifies for students the enormous and often overwhelming mass of material now available via print and electronic media. Collected in every volume is an array of opinions that captures the essence of a particular controversy or topic. Introducing Issues with Opposing Viewpoints books embody the spirit of nineteenth-century journalist Charles A. Dana's axiom: "Fight for your opinions, but do not believe that they contain the whole truth, or the only truth." Absorbing such contrasting opinions teaches students to analyze the strength of an argument and compare it to its opposition. From this process readers can inform and strengthen their own opinions, or be exposed to new information that will change their minds. Introducing Issues with Opposing Viewpoints is a mosaic of different voices. The authors are statesmen, pundits, academics, journalists, corporations, and ordinary people who have felt compelled to share their experiences and ideas in a public forum. Their words have been collected from newspapers, journals, books, speeches, interviews, and the Internet, the fastest growing body of opinionated material in the world.

Introducing Issues with Opposing Viewpoints shares many of the well-known features of its critically acclaimed parent series, Opposing Viewpoints. The articles are presented in a pro/con format, allowing readers to absorb divergent perspectives side by side. Active reading questions preface each viewpoint, requiring the student to approach the material thoughtfully and carefully. Useful charts, graphs, and cartoons supplement each article. A thorough introduction provides readers with crucial background on an issue. An annotated bibliography points the reader toward articles, books, and websites that contain additional information on the topic. An appendix of organizations to contact contains a wide variety of charities, nonprofit organizations, political groups, and private enterprises that each hold a position on the issue at hand. Finally, a comprehensive index allows readers to locate content quickly and efficiently.

Introducing Issues with Opposing Viewpoints is also significantly different from Opposing Viewpoints. As the series title implies, its presentation will help introduce students to the concept of opposing viewpoints and learn to use this material to aid in critical writing and debate. The series' four-color, accessible format makes the books attractive and inviting to readers of all levels. In addition, each viewpoint has been carefully edited to maximize a reader's understanding of the content. Short but thorough viewpoints capture the essence of an argument. A substantial, thought-provoking essay question placed at the end of each viewpoint asks the student to further investigate the issues raised in the viewpoint, compare and contrast two authors' arguments, or consider how one might go about forming an opinion on the topic at hand. Each viewpoint contains sidebars that include at-a-glance information and handy statistics. A Facts About section located in the back of the book further supplies students with relevant facts and figures.

Following in the tradition of the Opposing Viewpoints series, Greenhaven Press continues to provide readers with invaluable exposure to the controversial issues that shape our world. As John Stuart Mill once wrote: "The only way in which a human being can make some approach to knowing the whole of a subject is by hearing what can be said about it by persons of every variety of opinion and studying all modes in which it can be looked at by every character of mind. No wise man ever acquired his wisdom in any mode but this." It is to this principle that Introducing Issues with Opposing Viewpoints books are dedicated.

Introduction

"Plastic surgery is one of those complicated things that can be extremely polarizing. It's not something we should make light of or something we should be judgmental about either. It's unrealistic to believe that we don't live in a culture that adores and privileges a certain kind of beauty. It's also pretty ridiculous that about 99% of humans don't fit into that very specific mold."

—Emerald Pellot, "15 Celebrities Who Say 'YOLO' to Plastic Surgery," *College Candy*, 2013

Every year, millions of women and men select surgical treatments to enhance, minimize, nip, and tuck all manner of physical features. According to the American Society of Plastic Surgeons (ASPS), "14.6 million cosmetic plastic surgery procedures, including both minimally-invasive and surgical, were performed in the United States in 2012, up 5 percent since 2011."[1] From face-lifts, tummy tucks, and breast augmentation to liposuction, laser hair removal, and Botox injections, there is a procedure out there that can repair, remove, lift, and smooth just about every inch of the human body.

Media manipulation of the appearance of photographic subjects regularly occurs, feeding society with unattainable ideals and encouraging people to mutilate themselves for psychological reasons. According to the blog *Beauty Redefined*:

> While representations of women's bodies across the media spectrum have shrunk dramatically in the last three decades, rates of eating disorders have skyrocketed—tripling for college-age women from the late '80s to 1993 and rising since then to 4% suffering with bulimia. . . . Perhaps even more startling is the 119 percent increase in the number of children under age 12 hospitalized due to an eating disorder between 1999 and 2006, the vast majority of whom were girls."[2]

Physical imperfections do not upset everyone who has them, of course. But for some, they can shape a poor self-image and decrease already-low confidence levels. Some men, women, and teens find that their physical flaws seriously limit their social interaction and personal success and have an effect on their overall self-satisfaction. While this is a common issue, when taken to the level of an obsession it can become a serious problem and is likely more a matter of mental health than an issue of physical appearance. "Social platforms like Instagram, Snapchat and the iPhone app Selfie.im, which are solely image based, force patients to hold a microscope up to their own image and often look at it with a more self-critical eye than ever before," says American Academy of Facial Plastic and Reconstructive Surgery president Edward Farrior. "These images are often the first impressions young people put out there to prospective friends, romantic interests and employers and our patients want to put their best face forward."[3]

There is a rising number of teenagers undergoing cosmetic surgery. While adults generally use cosmetic surgery to stand out, many teens desire it in order to fit in with their peers. According to ASPS:

Not every teenager seeking plastic surgery is well suited for an operation. Teens must demonstrate emotional maturity and an understanding of the limitations of plastic surgery. The ASPS cautions teenagers and parents to keep in mind that plastic surgery is real surgery, with great benefits, but also carries some risks. Teens should have realistic expectations about plastic surgery and what it can do for them. In addition, certain milestones in growth and physical maturity must be achieved before undergoing plastic surgery.[4]

So how do people weigh the pros and cons of cosmetic surgery and make informed, balanced decisions about their beauty and long-term well-being? First, they must consider very carefully the benefits and drawbacks of the surgery they are interested in. Before plunging headlong into cosmetic surgery it is important to consider one's mental state, not just what one sees as one's physical shortcomings. Sometimes outer appearance can seem like the main problem when in reality, it is what is inside that is making the person feel insecure.

Anyone deliberating whether to undergo a cosmetic procedure must first make a careful and objective review of her or his goals, expectations, and needs. Not every patient will react the same way to the same surgery even with the same surgeon. A satisfied cosmetic surgery patient is one who understands that even a positive result will come with some drawbacks.

A number of deterring factors need to be considered as well, such as a patient's current health condition, recovery rates, infection risks, and the risk of becoming addicted to cosmetic surgery. People who have current heart conditions, diabetes, or are overweight are at the greatest risk for negative consequences. In order to clarify all the possible outcomes of cosmetic surgery, whether good or bad, the candidate for such surgery should consult a doctor before planning any such surgery. This allows one to assess the risks involved and to determine whether any medications one is taking might cause complications. With cosmetic surgeries, results may be unrealistic or not up to the expectations of the person undergoing the surgery.

Introducing Issues with Opposing Viewpoints: Cosmetic Surgery explores the potential benefits and consequences of cosmetic surgery. Authors in this anthology debate whether such surgery is safe, beneficial or detrimental, and for everyone or just certain people.

Notes

1. American Society of Plastic Surgeons, "14.6 Million Cosmetic Plastic Surgery Procedures Performed in 2012," Plasticsurgery .org, February 19, 2013. www.plasticsurgery.org/news/past -press-releases/2013-archives/14-million-cosmetic-plastic -surgery-procedures-performed-in-2012.html.
2. Lindsay Kite and Lexie Kite, "Photoshopping: Altering Images and Our Minds," *Beauty Redefined* (blog), March 12, 2014. www.beautyredefined.net/photoshopping-altering-images-and -our-minds/.
3. Quoted in Victoria Taylor, "Selfies Are Motivating Young People to Get Plastic Surgery: Poll," NYDailyNews.com, March 13, 2014. www.nydailynews.com/life-style/selfies-sparking-rise -plastic-surgery-poll-article-1.1720973.
4. American Society of Plastic Surgeons, "Plastic Surgery for Teenagers," briefing paper, no date. www.plasticsurgery.org/news /briefing-papers/plastic-surgery-for-teenagers.html.

Chapter 1

Is Cosmetic Surgery Safe?

A plastic surgeon shows a silicone implant to a patient. Well-informed patients meet with their plastic surgeon prior to the procedure to discuss options, safety measures, and after-care procedures.

The Hidden Dangers of Plastic Surgery

Jenna Goudreau

"Many patients do not fully grasp the gravity or potential risks of these operations."

In the following viewpoint, Jenna Goudreau contends that many cosmetic surgery patients do not fully understand the dangers of these operations. The author details the various physical, emotional, and cultural side effects that patients should consider before having such surgery. She highlights instances of botched surgeries. In addition she explores the emotional arc that occurs after such surgery. Although the number of cosmetic surgeries is on the rise, the author maintains that patients should think twice before having cosmetic surgical procedures. Goudreau is a staff writer for *Forbes*, a finance magazine, who has also written for *Businessweek*, *Ladies' Home Journal*, and others.

AS YOU READ, CONSIDER THE FOLLOWING QUESTIONS:

1. Women make up what percentage of all cosmetic surgery patients, as stated by the author?
2. According to Goudreau, what happens to women who suction fat from their thighs and lower abdomen?
3. As stated by the author, what is the general emotional arc after surgery?

Jenna Goudreau, "The Hidden Dangers of Plastic Surgery." From *Forbes*, June 16, 2011. Copyright © 2011 Forbes LLC. All rights reserved. Used by permission and protected by the Copyright Laws of the United States. The printing, copying, redistribution, or retransmission of this Content without express written permission is prohibited.

Cosmetic surgery has become a booming, $10.1 billion business each year in the U.S., according to the American Society of Plastic Surgeons. Women, already 91% of cosmetic patients, are electing to make these quick fixes more than ever, undergoing 5% more procedures in 2010 than the year before.

And it's not just a nip and tuck to appear younger and fresher: Greater numbers of young women are now going under the knife. Cosmetic procedures are up 4% for women in their 30s, and 30%

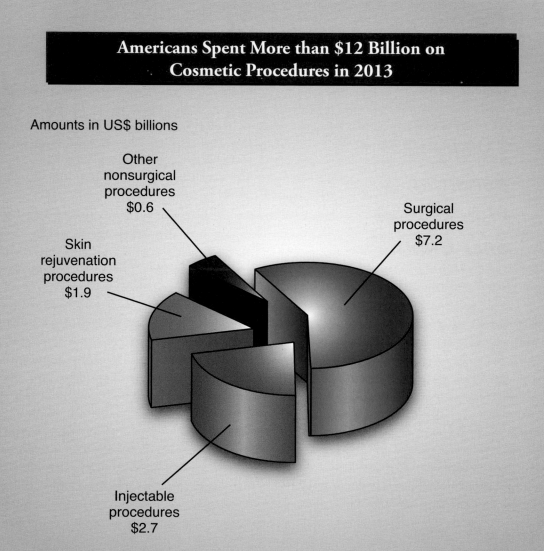

Americans Spent More than $12 Billion on Cosmetic Procedures in 2013

Amounts in US$ billions

Other nonsurgical procedures $0.6

Surgical procedures $7.2

Skin rejuvenation procedures $1.9

Injectable procedures $2.7

Taken from: Cosmetic Surgery National Data Bank Statistics, "Economic, Regional, and Ethnic Information," American Society for Aesthetic Plastic Surgery, 2013.

of all liposuction recipients are ages 19 to 34, reports the American Society for Aesthetic Plastic Surgery. It may indicate a new wave of perfection-seekers, as normal-weight women trim an inch of unwanted fat from their thighs or ditch their miracle bras for larger breasts—now the most popular invasive procedure.

However, psychologists and surgeons fear that many patients do not fully grasp the gravity or potential risks of these operations. "People think it's like going out to lunch," says Anne Wallace, chief of plastic surgery at University of California, San Diego Health System. "Like any surgery, it needs to be taken seriously."

FAST FACT

According to the American Society for Aesthetic Plastic Surgery, the most common cosmetic surgery procedure in the United States in 2013 was liposuction.

Experts detail the full spectrum of unintended physical, emotional and cultural side effects that may make you think twice about taking nature into your own hands.

Any time you tamper with the body's balance, you risk creating new problem areas, says Wallace. In other words: Be careful what you wish for.

One recent study found that liposuction may slim one problem area while creating another. Women who suction fat from their thighs and lower abdomen ultimately destroy those fat cells. When they eventually put weight back on, it distributes unevenly—often to less flattering areas like the upper abdomen, back and arms.

Similarly, Wallace warns that changing one feature sometimes throws off the appearance of others. A tummy tuck may cause the thighs to look out of proportion, while plumped lips may make a normal sized nose suddenly appear obtrusive. She's seen cases where Botox injections, which paralyze certain facial muscles, caused the other active muscles to appear strangely overpowering and "odd."

Scarier still are the potential deformities. Marilyn Leisz thought she was undergoing a simple procedure to her eyes; 30 surgeries later she is still unable to blink. Meanwhile, a botched face-lift severely damaged the nerves of British businesswoman Penny Johnson, who lost her business and became a recluse.

A hidden danger of cosmetic surgery is the emotional damage a patient could experience from a procedure.

If there is a problem and the patient is not emotionally stable or financially secure, "the results can be disastrous," says Robin Yuan, plastic surgeon and author of *Behind the Mask, Beneath the Glitter*. A person who is already insecure about an aspect of their appearance may suffer a severe blow to their confidence if the surgery goes awry. At the same time, Yuan says many patients borrow money for the initial surgery. If they need an additional procedure, follow-up costs can devastate their financial lives.

Threats Below the Surface

Patients may never be fully prepared for the mental and emotional costs of cosmetic surgery, says Joseph Hullett, a psychiatrist and senior medical director of OptumHealth. The stress of surgery, lack of sleep and recuperation that often includes pain, fatigue and swelling causes most to experience some degree of depression. "If you have a face-lift, you really look like a beaten-up fighter. It becomes real," he says. And with all the related side effects, "your whole life may start to unravel."

According to Hullett, the general emotional arc after surgery begins with depression as you heal, then shifts to a honeymoon phase when you can see the result but soon morphs into some measure of disappointment. Those that fantasized the physical change would result in more attention, a promotion or attractive partner are often let down by the reality. Moreover, their expectations of beauty may rise, says Hullett. Even if the procedure was an improvement, they become deeply disappointed when the result isn't "perfect."

Sometimes a patient—or her doctor—may realize after they've invested the money and time into a procedure that they have an underlying issue rather than a physical one. Someone with body dysmorphic disorder, BDD, exaggerates a flaw to the point of delusion, imagining a minor imperfection as a hideous disfigurement. After surgery, they may simply become fixated on another body part. "They develop a new obsession," Hullett says. "They get the nose fixed, and then it's the eyebrows. They fix the eyebrows, and then it's the ears. The perceived abnormality keeps moving."

Perhaps the most insidious threat of a cosmetic change is the response by others. "You can't control the way others react," warns Yuan. He once had a patient, a young mother in her 20s, who got a breast augmentation. She was thrilled with the results but had not expected that her suburban-mom peer group would disapprove and make her feel uncomfortable about her new body. She returned six months later and had the implants removed.

At the same time, those that undergo a procedure to gain an edge at work may be stunned to realize that it has instead alienated colleagues. Coworkers may perceive you as vain, manipulative or threatening. Other men may interpret a male colleague's new head of hair as an unfair advantage, or women may decide a female's new, larger breasts are an abuse of sexual power. Rather than the toast of the water cooler, "they might become the subject of office gossip," says Hullett.

Finally, the hidden hazards within the family may be worst of all. Children who watch a parent or close relative take the drastic measure of surgery can develop a skewed vision of their own bodies that they may never escape. Likewise, women who hope a procedure will help their romantic relationship often receive a rude awakening. According to Hullett, men are especially apt to misunderstand a woman's motives, believing her to be dissatisfied or interested in attracting other men. In fact, he's seen more relationships fail rather than flourish after one partner undergoes a major physical change.

EVALUATING THE AUTHOR'S ARGUMENTS

In this viewpoint, Jenna Goudreau claims that many patients do not fully grasp the potential risks of cosmetic surgery. What hazards would Goudreau advise patients to research before undergoing surgery? Do you agree with her argument? Why or why not?

Cosmetic Surgery Can Be Safe

"[Various] cosmetic dermatology surgical procedures . . . are well-known to be safe and effective."

Marla Paul

In the following viewpoint, Marla Paul contends that there are safe cosmetic surgery treatments available for patients; however, she believes that many consumers are often unaware of the safest and most effective cosmetic procedures. The author highlights several common procedures and examines their effectiveness and safety. It is vital for consumers to select an experienced practitioner, she maintains, and research the many different types of treatment available. Paul is a health sciences editor at Northwestern University in Evanston, Illinois.

AS YOU READ, CONSIDER THE FOLLOWING QUESTIONS:

1. According to the author, the cosmetic dermatology industry brings in how much annual revenue in the United States?
2. What does noninvasive skin tightening use to heat and shrink the skin, according to Paul?
3. Companies generally test a new device on how many patients, as stated by the author?

Marla Paul, "Cosmetic Surgery and Treatments: How Safe Are They?," Women's Health Research Institute at Northwestern University, January 2012. Copyright © 2012 by Marla Paul. All rights reserved. Reproduced by permission.

I s it more effective to freeze your love handles, killing the fat cells between two super-cooled plates in a procedure known as cryolipolysis, or vacuum them away with liposuction? And which lasts longer, a surgical facelift or facial skin tightening via a laser?

Consumers often are in the dark about the most effective and safest cosmetic dermatology procedures to improve skin texture and color and remove subcutaneous fat, a surging $10 billion industry in the United States. One reason is a dearth of comparable research trials, reports a new Northwestern Medicine study. The study, published in the January [2012] issue of the journal *Dermatologic Clinics*, reviews existing research and identifies which procedures have been proven safe and effective and which ones have less evidence behind them.

Comparing the Safety of Cosmetic Treatments

"Many treatments gaining popularity are novel techniques that use complex devices, such as lasers and ultrasound, but there is sparse research evaluating their long-term effects," said lead author Murad Alam, MD, chief of cutaneous and aesthetic surgery at Northwestern University Feinberg School of Medicine. "We need more prospective studies comparing different treatments for the same problem head-to-head, so doctors and consumers know what's best and safest.". . .

> **FAST FACT**
>
> *Psychology Today* reports that 78 percent of plastic surgery patients said they were still "extremely satisfied" two years after their procedure.

Alam said the cosmetic dermatology surgical procedures that are well-known to be safe and effective when done by a trained, board-certified physician include: injected neurotoxins to smooth wrinkles; liposuction to remove fat; and lasers to treat broken blood vessels, port wine stains and rosacea and for removing brown spots and hair. . . .

Other procedures that may be effective but have less evidence behind them include devices that use infrared light or ultrasound to purportedly shrink and tighten the skin, low-level laser light for fat removal, and fat "melting" by super cooling the fat cells, Alam noted.

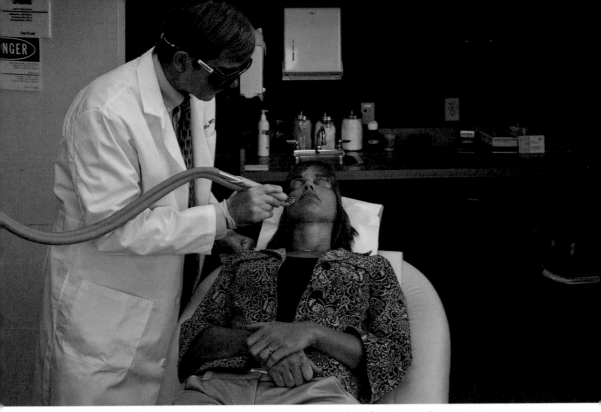

A physician performs a laser treatment to remove or reduce facial imperfections. Many cosmetic surgery procedures have proven track records of being safe and effective when performed by a board-certified doctor.

These are approved by the Food and Drug Administration (FDA), and data show they work and are safe short term. But these procedures are newer and therefore less is known about their long-term safety and effectiveness.

"Patients need to be smart consumers and ask their doctors better questions, such as, 'How does procedure A compare to procedure B?'" Alam said. "Is there research comparing treatments, such as a facelift versus non-invasive skin tightening? Is there evidence regarding the degree of improvement and how long the results will last? How long has a particular procedure or device been approved, and would the doctor be comfortable recommending it to a friend or family member?'"

Common Procedures

Injectable botulinum toxins type A or neurotoxins: "These have been around for 20 years and during that entire period, when an approved

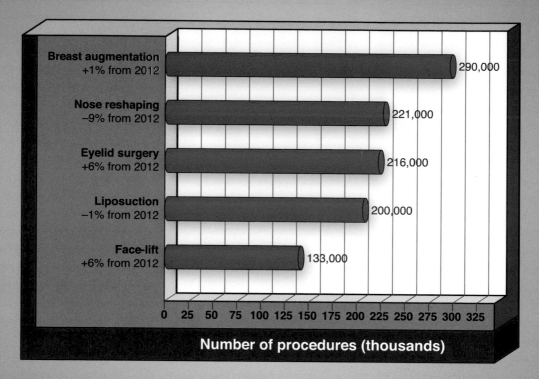

Top Five Cosmetic Surgical Procedures in 2013

Breast augmentation
+1% from 2012 — 290,000

Nose reshaping
−9% from 2012 — 221,000

Eyelid surgery
+6% from 2012 — 216,000

Liposuction
−1% from 2012 — 200,000

Face-lift
+6% from 2012 — 133,000

0 25 50 75 100 125 150 175 200 225 250 275 300 325

Number of procedures (thousands)

Note: Data from American Society of Plastic Surgeons

Taken from: Alexandra Sifferlin, "Here Are the Most Popular Plastic Surgery Procedures in Three Charts," *Time*, February 26, 2014.

pharmaceutical product in approved doses is used for cosmetic purposes, there have not been any instances of serious reactions," Alam reported.

Liposuction: "Tumescent liposuction, the kind when you inject fluid into the area where you are removing fat, has been shown to be exceedingly safe," Alam said. "The main potential complication, excessive bleeding, simply doesn't occur with that form of liposuction when appropriate rules are followed because the anesthetic used in the procedure prevents bleeding."

Low-level laser light for fat removal: "Some companies sell products they claim can cause changes in skin and subcutaneous tissue," Alam said. "One of these devices has been approved for reducing fat. It's safe, but we have very limited information about its degree of effectiveness or how long the result lasts."

Fat freezing: A device sandwiches the fat on the abdomen or thighs between two cooling plates. The fat cells die and are absorbed by the body. "It's FDA approved and does work,"Alam said, "but we don't know how long it lasts or how many cubic centimeters of fat will go away in different patients. While it appears to be safe and is a promising treatment, we won't know for several more years if there is a downside or if fat removal is truly permanent."

Non-invasive skin tightening: These devices use radio-frequency energy or infrared light or ultrasound to heat and shrink the skin. "Some tightening definitely occurs," Alam said. "What we don't know is exactly how much tightening goes on, who it will work on or how long it will last." One study compared facelifts to these minimally invasive methods and found that they provided approximately one-third the tightening benefits of surgical facelifts.

Obstacles to Big Research Trials

Several obstacles prevent conducting large-scale research trials on cosmetic procedures and devices, Alam said. Because the FDA's approval mechanism for devices is less rigorous than for drugs, the agency doesn't compel pharmaceutical companies to do large trials. Thus, companies may test a device on as few as 50 or 100 patients. As soon as a mechanism gets approval, companies aren't motivated to do more testing or to compare one procedure to another.

Nor is there government funding for cosmetic surgery trials. Recently, the FDA asked companies with recently approved devices to continue monitoring patients even after approval to make sure no new problems are uncovered later.

Finding the Right Treatment

"Selecting the right cosmetic treatment for a patient is not a trivial matter," Alam stressed. "Patients should get treatments from experienced practitioners with access to the data and an ability to evaluate it, rather than someone at a nearby spa who just has one laser, is minimally trained and is not able to evaluate the scientific evidence but eager to use this device for every patient complaint."

Patients should be aware there are often many different types of treatment for the same cosmetic concern, Alam said. One of these may be most appropriate for the patient's specific issues and personal preferences (such as degree of downtime that is tolerable). "Experienced physicians can help patients select the treatments that are best for them," he noted.

To find a skilled cosmetic dermatologist, patients can look for members of major dermatology associations, such as the American Academy of Dermatology or the American Society for Dermatologic Surgery. Association websites will often provide contact information about such physicians in a specific geographic area. It is also useful to ask physicians if they have specific training in cosmetic dermatologic surgery and what types of procedures they do often.

EVALUATING THE AUTHOR'S ARGUMENTS

In this viewpoint, Marla Paul claims that patients should select an experienced cosmetic surgeon and research the many different types of cosmetic treatments available for their concern. Do you think she would agree with Jenna Goudreau about the dangers of cosmetic surgery? Why or why not?

Breast Implants Can Cause Health Problems

Nalini Chilkov

"There are serious life threatening and life altering . . . risks associated with breast implants."

In the following viewpoint, Nalini Chilkov argues that breast implants can cause numerous life-threatening outcomes for patients. The author urges consumers to research the potential risks of breast augmentation surgery before undergoing the procedure. She explores potential negative outcomes of such surgery, from infection to disfigurement, metal poisoning, and the development of various autoimmune diseases. Breast implants compromise women's health, the author contends, and the surgery is not worth the risk. Chilkov is a doctor of Oriental medicine and works in the field of integrative cancer care and prevention; she is the creator of IntegrativeCancerAnswers.com.

AS YOU READ, CONSIDER THE FOLLOWING QUESTIONS:

1. According to the author, what are the causes of infection from breast implants?
2. Chilkov states that which autoimmune diseases are linked to breast implants?

Nalini Chilkov, "25 Reasons Not to Get Breast Implants," *Huffington Post*, February 1, 2011. Copyright © 2011 by The Huffington Post. All rights reserved. Reproduced by permission.

Last week [January 2011] the FDA [US Food and Drug Administration] reported that breast implants put women's lives in danger. The big news last week was that a small number of women can get a very rare type of cancer (ALCL: anaplastic large cell lymphoma). It confirmed that death is a possible side effect of breast implants.

But what no one is talking about are all the other more frequent, more common and very real dangers and problems that go along with breast implants. Does the FDA really believe that if we don't kill too many women it's acceptable to disfigure them and compromise women's health in other less lethal ways?

Understanding the Risks of Surgery

According to Diana Zuckerman, Ph.D., Elizabeth Nagelin-Anderson, M.A., and Elizabeth Santoro, R.N., M.P.H.:

> In 2008, more than 300,000 women and teenagers underwent surgery to have their breasts enlarged with silicone or saline implants, and almost 80,000 breast cancer patients had reconstruction after mastectomy, often with implants. The popularity of breast augmentation has more than tripled since 1997, when there were just over 101,000 of these procedures. More than 40,000 implant removal procedures were also reported in 2008.

FAST FACT

The FDA reports that 20 percent of patients with breast implants have them removed within eight to ten years because of complications.

Take a look at the list below and decide if you would let someone you love take these risks with their health . . . just to have a bigger boobs . . . What price are women willing to pay? Why are women so unhappy with their breasts? Do we really think we will be loved more if we have a bigger bra size? Maybe men could let us know

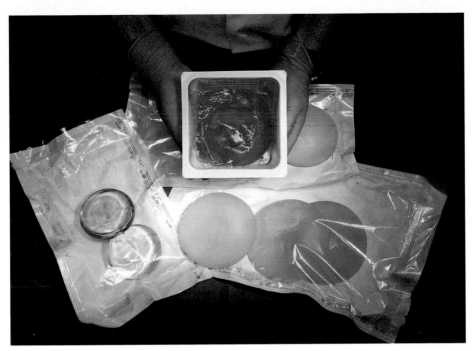

A plastic surgeon holds a ruptured breast implant that was removed from a patient. A ruptured implant is one of several complications that can arise from a breast augmentation procedure.

how lovely small breasts really are. Hey guys . . . step up to and save some women's lives. Tell us we are beautiful and you love us with any size breasts and that you would rather have us healthy than sick, alive, not dead.

Now I agree, a breast cancer survivor is justified in wanting her disfigured body restored to symmetry and wholeness. But does she really want to risk another cancer and more surgeries? And what about healthy women who go under the knife willingly?

Stop, take a breath and understand the real risks and the possible complications. Get educated. Get smart. Look before you leap.

Examining the Harm Caused by Breast Implants

Here is what can happen to you with breast implants excerpted from *What You Need to Know About Breast Implants* published by the National Research Center for Women and Families. This publication also has a long list of research and references to support the following statements:

Russell Memorial Library
88 Main Street
Acushnet, MA 02743

Complications of Breast Surgery and Silicone and Saline Breast Implants include:

- infection (bacteria and mold which can be released from the implant into the body)
- surgical risks
- anesthesia risks
- chronic breast pain
- breast or nipple numbness
- capsular contracture
- scar tissue
- hardened and misshapen breasts
- breakage and leakage
- necrosis (skin death)
- need for additional surgery to deal with problems
- dissatisfaction with how the breast looks
- disfigurement
- arthritis and joint pain
- fatigue
- memory loss
- cognitive impairment: poor concentration
- metal poisoning due to platinum exposure (in silicone implants)
- silicone migration into lymph nodes and other organs
- debilitating autoimmune disease such as fibromyalgia, dermatomyositis, polymyositis, Hashimoto's thyroiditis, mixed connective-tissue disease, pulmonary fibrosis, eosinophilic fasciitis, and polymyalgia
- And last but not least, death

Additionally, *it is harder to breastfeed* (if at all), and *harder to detect breast cancer.* Conscientious women having regular breast cancer screenings have had their *implants rupture from the pressure of a mammogram.*

Complications After Surgery Are Common

Within the first three years, approximately three out of four reconstruction (breast cancer) patients and almost half of first-time augmentation patients experienced at least one local complication—such as pain, infection, hardening, or the need for additional surgery.

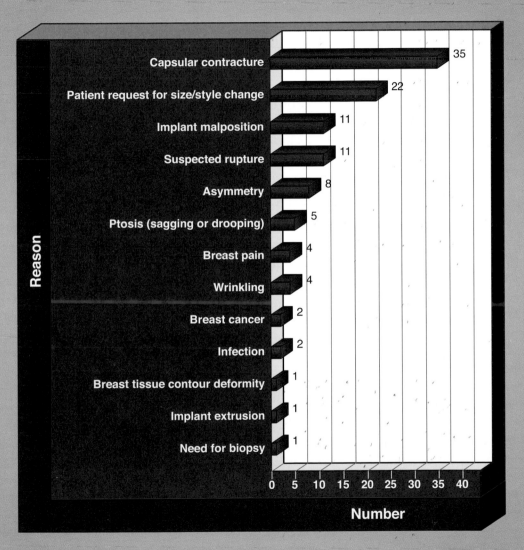

Main Reasons for Silicone Breast Implant Removal

Reason

Reason	Number
Capsular contracture	35
Patient request for size/style change	22
Implant malposition	11
Suspected rupture	11
Asymmetry	8
Ptosis (sagging or drooping)	5
Breast pain	4
Wrinkling	4
Breast cancer	2
Infection	2
Breast tissue contour deformity	1
Implant extrusion	1
Need for biopsy	1

Number

Note: Data for seven years after primary augmentation. N = 107. Data from the Allergan Core Study, a ten-year study on Natrelle silicone-filled breast implants with a total of 715 patients.

Taken from: Allergan, "Breast Augmentation with Natrelle Silicone-Filled Breast Implants," April 6, 2009, p. 30.

All breast implants will eventually break, but it is not known how many years the breast implants that are currently on the market will last. Studies of silicone breast implants suggest that most implants last 7–12 years, but some break during the first few months or years, while others last more than 15 years.

In a study conducted by FDA scientists, most women had at least one broken implant within 11 years, and the likelihood of rupture increases every year. Silicone-7 migrated outside of the breast capsule for 21 percent of the women, even though most women were unaware that this had happened.

Don't forget the financial burden and increased health insurance costs that go with multiple surgeries and medical complications. In some cases the surgery to remove implants can be like a mastectomy, complete removal of the breast tissue and sometimes the muscle underneath.

Additionally, quality of life is greatly compromised if you have chronic health problems as a result of complications from implants.

Take Home Lesson One: There are serious life threatening and life altering short term and long term health, cosmetic and economic risks associated with breast implants.

Take Home Lesson Two: Consider loving the body Mother Nature gave you rather than playing Russian Roulette with your health and your life.

EVALUATING THE AUTHOR'S ARGUMENTS

In this viewpoint, Nalini Chilkov claims that breast implants are dangerous to women. On the basis of her arguments, do you believe it is worth it for women to undergo breast surgery? Why or why not?

Breast Implants Do Not Cause Health Problems

Juliana Hansen

"Breast implants are not inherently dangerous."

In the following viewpoint, Juliana Hansen argues that breast implants do not endanger the health of women. The author dispels several beliefs about breast enhancement surgery, including assertions that breast implants cause cancer and make it difficult for women to breast-feed. She explores advances in breast-implant technology and details the makeup of the two types of implants used today. The author believes that the debate about breast-implant safety highlights the importance of making medical decisions and health policy on the basis of scientific research. Hansen is a surgeon and has served as the chief of plastic and reconstructive surgery at Oregon Health and Science University in Portland, Oregon, since 2000.

AS YOU READ, CONSIDER THE FOLLOWING QUESTIONS:

1. According to the author, are women with breast implants able to breast-feed safely?
2. What is the purpose of the breast-implant shell, as stated by Hansen?

Juliana Hansen, "Breast Implants: What We Now Know," Cancerconnect.com, March 2009. Copyright © 2009 by OMNI Health Media. All rights reserved. Reproduced by permission.

Breast implants. In the roughly 50 years since they first took the medical stage, they have been applauded, banned, modified, filled with different substances, and studied extensively. They have been the reason for the bankruptcy of a major company, the subject of a $4.2 billion settlement, the mainstay of cosmetic breast

A chest x-ray shows a patient after breast implant surgery. It is recommended that women with implants undergo some type of imaging every few years, to check implants for ruptures.

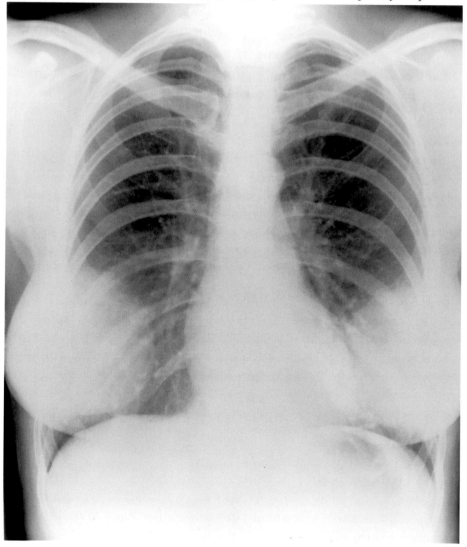

surgery, and an essential component of reconstructive breast surgery. They have generated headlines, lawsuits, myths, and millions of satisfied customers. Throughout this saga, they have been used without restrictions or hesitations everywhere in the world except the United States. So what has a half century taught us about breast implants, and what should women considering their use know today?

Myths About Breast Implants

Let's start with the myths that can be easily dispelled.

- Implants cause cancer. FALSE. *Breast implants do not cause cancer.*
- Implants make people sick. FALSE. *Breast implants do not cause other diseases.*
- Women with implants shouldn't breast-feed. FALSE. *Breast implants do not place breast-feeding babies or their mothers at risk.*
- Implants are dangerous. FALSE. *Breast implants are not inherently dangerous, though any surgical procedure can have complications and should be performed by a qualified practitioner. . . .*

Advances in Technology

Today breast implants have a thin, pliable sheet of silicone that encases the silicone gel filling. The shell keeps the gel material contained and prevents direct contact with the breast tissue. But this safe, effective model is not the only idea developers of implants have devised. Since 1963, when the first generation of implants was released, a number of different types have been created, varying in the type of shell used and in the material filling the shell (vegetable oil was even studied as a possible filler but was abandoned when it was found to go rancid). Ultimately, no other filler has proved equal to silicone. It is the silicone model that millions of women throughout

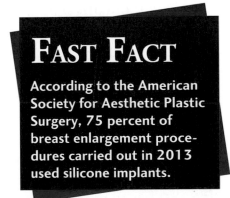

FAST FACT

According to the American Society for Aesthetic Plastic Surgery, 75 percent of breast enlargement procedures carried out in 2013 used silicone implants.

the world have opted to use for both augmentation and reconstructive purposes. . . .

Two types of implants currently exist: silicone implants and saline implants. Both types have a shell made of silicone, formed from a thin layer of a pliable but solid form of silicone. They differ in the material used to fill the shell. Silicone implants are filled with a gel form of silicone, which is thick and squishy with a consistency like bread dough. Saline implants are filled with saltwater and have a consistency more like a water balloon. Both types are widely used, and both have advantages. Silicone implants have a more natural feel and blend in better with natural tissue.

Saline implants do not present the same concern for leaks as silicone implants do, so there are no recommendations for routine monitoring or exchange. They are the only implants available for women under the age of 22. Saline implants have always been available for women of all ages, even throughout the silicone implant ban. Both silicone and saline implants come in a variety of sizes, diameters, and projections. They come in either a smooth form or a textured surface and are either round or "anatomically" shaped, with a narrower top and a fuller bottom. Surgeons tend to have preferences for implants based on what they feel (in their hands) will give their patients the nicest results and have the lowest chance of complications.

Possible Complications with Implants

What have we learned about implant leak and rupture? The longer an implant has been in place, the more likely a leak or rupture is to occur. Factors that may influence rupture include stress on the implant during insertion, scarring around the implant, folds that create weak points, and severe external pressure or trauma to the chest. A leak may not be obvious with silicone implants, which is why doctors call this occurrence a "silent rupture." Women who have undergone screening tests with magnetic resonance imaging (MRI) to look for signs of leak show a 0.5 percent incidence of rupture at three years for augmentation patients and 0.9 percent among reconstruction patients. Some women experience symptoms associated with rupture, such as knots surrounding the implant, lumps in the armpit, a change in breast appearance, or a hardening, tingling, burning, or numbness of the

Saline vs. Silicone Breast Implants

	Silicone	Saline
Minimum age of patient	22	18
Material	Filled with silicone gel	Filled with sterile salt water
Filling	Pre-filled	Filled after placement
Placement options	Over or under pectoral muscle	Over or under pectoral muscle
Results	More natural feel with lower chance of rippling	Harder feel with greater chance of rippling
Longevity	15–20 years	7–10 years
Rupturing	Not absorbed by body and remains in breast implant pocket	Implant will collapse and body will absorb the saline solution

Taken from: "Comparing Silicone, Saline, and 'Gummy Bear' Breast Implants: Infographic," Barbara L. Persons, MD–Persons Plastic Surgery, February 20, 2013.

breast. To date, the data available from multiple studies show that when leakage occurs, the problems remain localized to the breast and nearby lymph nodes.

When a woman suspects an implant rupture, she should seek a medical evaluation that includes a physical exam and imaging (likely an MRI or ultrasound). If a rupture is confirmed, the implant should be removed and exchanged. The current recommendations for silicone implants are to undergo routine screening tests for rupture. The FDA has established guidelines that include a first MRI at three years post-implantation followed by every two years. Recommendations also include a preventive implant exchange every 10 years. It is not yet clear if this will prove to be the best way to screen for leaks or prevent problems related to ruptured implants.

Saline implants are different from silicone when it comes to rupture. If they leak, the body quickly and safely reabsorbs the saltwater, and deflation becomes obvious. An implant may appear softer and less full, or it may deflate fully and flatten. In these cases, patients should undergo surgery to replace the implant as soon as it is convenient, although there are no health-related concerns.

Both types of implants normally develop a capsule of scar tissue around them. When this scar tissue becomes thickened and squeezes on an implant, a condition called capsular contracture develops. In and of itself, this condition is not dangerous, though it may cause an implant to change shape and appearance and become hard. In severe cases capsular contracture may cause discomfort and would result in an additional surgery to repair or replace the implant.

Women who get implants tend to be very pleased with the results, but they should be aware that implants in general are not lifetime devices. After implantation it is likely that at some point they will need additional surgery. In one large study, 15 percent of women who underwent a first-time breast augmentation had additional surgery within three years. The main reason for this additional procedure was to repair scarring around the implant. The second most common reason patients had additional surgery was to change the size or shape of the implant. For women who had implants for reconstruction after breast cancer surgery, 27 percent underwent a second procedure within three years. Among these women the main reason for the second procedure was to address asymmetry.

Rely on Safe Medicine and Sound Data

The saga of silicone implants highlights the importance of medical decision-making and health policy that is based on fact and scientific data and not swayed by sensationalism, speculation, and widespread litigation. It also highlights the importance of safe utilization of medical innovations. Women considering implants should be sure that they are seeing a reputable surgeon, trained in plastic surgery, with whom they can work for immediate care as well as for long-term follow-up.

EVALUATING THE AUTHOR'S ARGUMENTS

In this viewpoint, Juliana Hansen claims that breast implants do not pose a danger to women. Whose evidence do you find more convincing, hers or Nalini Chilkov's in the preceding viewpoint? Explain your answer.

Having Cosmetic Surgery Abroad Is Risky

"For some women [having cosmetic surgery abroad] is the start of a nightmare."

Emma Pietras

In the following viewpoint, Emma Pietras contends that leaving the United Kingdom for cosmetic surgery is dangerous. The author argues that cosmetic surgery trips can lead to disastrous consequences and that one in five British patients needs corrective treatment upon returning home. She details the experiences of three patients who went abroad for cosmetic surgery and suffered from various related health complications. One patient developed a double chin, another was heavily scarred, and one nearly died. Pietras is a *Daily Mirror* feature writer who lives in London.

AS YOU READ, CONSIDER THE FOLLOWING QUESTIONS:

1. According to the author, how many British patients are unhappy with the results of cosmetic surgery they have had abroad?
2. How much does it cost to have a face-lift in the United Kingdom, according to Pietras?
3. What is necrosis, as described by the author?

Emma Pietras, "The Women Who Went Abroad for Cheap Cosmetic Surgery and Ended Up Scarred for Life," *Mirror Online*, Janurary 6, 2014. Copyright © 20014 by Mirrorpix. All rights reserved. Reproduced by permission.

S urgery holidays are booming and nearly a third of plastic surgery patients are now flocking abroad for a cut-price nip and tuck. But instead of returning home with improved looks, for some women the process is the start of a nightmare.

Nearly half of patients aren't happy with the results of their operations, with a worrying one in five needing corrective treatment when

Procedure Prices for Medical Tourism in Selected Countries

Costs of surgeries in US$

Procedure	Nose Job	Tummy Tuck	Breast Reduction	Breast Implants
United States	$4,500	$6,400	$5,200	$6,000
India	$2,000	$2,900	$2,500	$2,200
Thailand	$2,500	$3,500	$3,750	$2,600
Singapore	$4,375	$6,250	$8,000	$8,000
Malaysia	$2,083	$3,903	$3,343	$3,308
Mexico	$3,200	$3,000	$3,000	$2,500
Cuba	$1,535	$1,831	$1,668	$1,248
Poland	$1,700	$3,500	$3,146	$5,243
Hungary	$2,858	$3,136	$3,490	$3,871
UK	$3,500	$4,810	$5,075	$4,350

Note: Price comparisons take into account hospital and doctor charges, but do not include the costs of flights and hotel for the expected lengths of stay. Data compiled March 2011 from medical tourism providers and brokers online.

Taken from: Neil Lunt et al., "Medical Tourism: Treatments, Markets, and Health System Implications: A Scoping Review," Organisation for Economic Co-operation and Development, Directorate for Employment, Labour, and Social Affairs, 2011. www.oecd.org/els/health -systems/48723982.pdf.

they get back home, according to research carried out by price comparison website Confused.com. . . .

Cosmetic surgery coach Antonia Mariconda has seen first-hand the results of botched operations abroad and aggressive sales pitches from overseas clinics.

"I have been inundated with people who are really unhappy and don't know what to do.

"They put their trust in the medical profession," she says. "The sales representative will give you all sorts of unrealistic expectations and visions of a five star service and it's simply not the case."

Antonia, who has launched a campaign called Safety In Beauty advising people on how to enhance their bodies safely, admits there are good surgeons abroad but people need to choose carefully.

[Douglas McGeorge, a plastic-surgery consultant] agrees: "You wouldn't go on holiday without doing research on where you're staying. Why go abroad and not check what the surgeons are like first? It's the most basic thing to do."

These three readers all went abroad for cosmetic ops with disastrous consequences:

"I Developed a Double Chin After My Face-Lift"

Hairdresser and mum-of-one Cheryl Faunch, 61, from Colchester, Essex, paid £3,200 [$5,328] to have a face, neck and upper-eye lift in Poland last April [2013].

By the time I reached 60, if I looked in the mirror all I could see were saggy eyebags and heavy jowls. Having a facelift in the UK costs around £5,000 [$8,372], so I booked a Polish clinic through a cosmetic surgery travel agency. . . .

The hospital was very clean, but hardly anyone there spoke English. Luckily the surgeon had a translator.

I had a local anaesthetic so I can remember some of the operation, and I was awake for the liposuction on my jowls, and everything seemed fine. Afterwards, I was bandaged up and taken to my apartment, and even did some sightseeing.

I stayed for 10 days and went back to the hospital three times for checkups. On my last day I had my stitches out, but when I got home I noticed some stitches had been missed.

I went to see my dentist, who took them out free of charge. My face was bruised and swollen for six weeks, but when it went down my neck skin and jowls were still loose.

Too much had been taken off one eyebag, and not enough off the other. When you do a face-lift, you're supposed to lift the muscles underneath and the skin, but he'd only lifted the skin.

When I rang the travel company to complain, they tried to pass the buck, saying they were just the third party. I emailed the hospital, which offered to do it again for free if I paid for the flights.

It wasn't done properly in the first place, so I wouldn't go through it again.

I've got a scar from my temple down to the nape of my neck. My face looks worse in some ways than before I had it done, and I've now got a double chin when I bend down that I didn't have before.

FAST FACT

According to the Organisation for Economic Co-operation and Development, the most common treatments sought by medical tourists are dental care, cosmetic surgery, elective surgery, and fertility treatment.

I wish I hadn't gone abroad and I wish I hadn't used that company. I think the surgeon used an outdated technique. He even shaved my hair at the sides and it's still not fully grown back.

The NHS [National Health Service] would never correct it, and I've been quoted £6,400 [$10, 716] to fix it privately, which I don't have. It's been a waste of time and money.

"My Tummy's Not Flat and Op Nearly Killed Me"

Mum-of-three Sue Briddick, 52, who lives in Brighton, went to Turkey in 2011 to undergo a tummy tuck and breast uplift.

I wanted a tummy tuck because I had a lot of loose skin after having my children. I kept asking my GP [general practitioner] if I could get it done on the NHS but they wouldn't help me.

I couldn't afford to have the operation done privately in the UK because it would have cost £11,000 [$18,419]. So I researched it online and came across a company in Turkey which looked quite nice.

The sales representative suggested I get my breasts done too and I thought why not? She sold me a package deal for £3,600 [$6,028] with flights and accommodation on top. Most people stay in a hotel but I paid extra to stay in an apartment with a carer [caregiver].

The clinic also insisted I pay in cash. In hindsight, alarm bells should have rung.

After a four-hour journey, when I got there I changed my mind. I just wanted to go home. But they coaxed me into staying.

After the two-hour operation, I went to stay with the carer who wasn't medically trained and her apartment was covered in cat hair.

A few days later, I went back to the hospital to have my dressings changed and when the bandages came off I noticed the skin on my tummy had turned black. They told me it was bruising and it would go away.

Ads for plastic surgery are displayed at the entrance of a subway station in South Korea, a popular destination for medical tourists from other Asian countries.

It wasn't until I got back home a couple of days later and showed my husband he said my skin was dead. I was horrified.

Days later, my mum paid for me to see a private surgeon who told me I had to go to hospital or I'd die.

Every part of me the surgeon had touched had an infection called necrosis, where not enough blood gets to your body tissue so it dies.

They had to scrape off the dead flesh and take a skin graft from my thigh. I was in hospital for a month and I felt bad using the NHS but at the same time I was practically dying.

My tummy has been left badly scarred. The Turkish surgeon hadn't given me a breast uplift either but a reduction and implants instead. The clinic offered to put things right for free but I'd have to pay for flights and accommodation myself.

I've tried to see if they will give me compensation but my emails and calls have been ignored.

"The Scars on My Arms Kept Growing"

Nursery manager and mum-of-two Laura Green, 35, from Gravesend, Kent, was left with nerve damage after having a £3,500 [$5860] arm lift to remove 'bingo wings' in Brussels, Belgium, in 2009. . . .

The clinic in Brussels was nice, clean and modern. The surgeon marked my arms and I thought, 'Wow, they're going to look great.'

Then he told me that they didn't use an anaesthetic and instead gave you an overdose of sedative to put you to sleep—and I trusted them.

Then my worst nightmare happened. The surgeon obviously didn't give me enough sedative because although I couldn't feel them cutting my skin, I could feel a lot of pressure and pulling.

I couldn't speak to tell them, though, and when I came round, I was hysterical.

The next day, I got the Eurostar home.

My arms were bandaged but didn't actually look any different.

A couple of days later, I changed my bandages and the scar, which ran from my armpit down to my elbow, looked normal but my arms looked as big as before.

And when I went to London for a follow-up consultation two weeks later, my surgeon said it was nothing to worry about and to come back in three months.

In that time, my scars grew to 3.5cm in width and I developed burning, stabbing sensations, like electric shocks in my scars. I knew something wasn't right.

My GP couldn't do anything because I'd gone private and just gave me painkillers.

My Brussels surgeon offered to correct the problem for another £1,000 [$1,674] but I had already taken out a loan to have the operation in the first place. I felt absolutely lost and hopeless.

I couldn't go through the rest of my life with my arms like that and, in the end, I contacted a television programme looking for case studies that agreed to pay to correct it for me.

I had the operation six weeks ago and I'm so pleased with the results. They're much smaller and my old scar tissue has gone.

My new surgeon thought the clinic in Brussels didn't put me to sleep because it's cheaper to sedate you.

He didn't understand why glue was used instead of stitches but explained the surgeon had nicked my nerve, which was causing the pain.

It wasn't just in my mind and I wasn't going crazy.

I would never have surgery done abroad again. It's not safe.

EVALUATING THE AUTHOR'S ARGUMENTS

In this viewpoint, Emma Pietras tells the stories of three women who had bad experiences getting cosmetic surgery abroad and claims that it is risky for patients to have cosmetic surgery abroad. On the basis of the information in the viewpoint, would you travel abroad for surgery to save money? Why or why not?

Chapter 2

Is Cosmetic Surgery Beneficial or Harmful?

Justin Jedica is known as the human "Ken" doll because of the numerous cosmetic surgeries he has undergone in a quest to achieve the perfect physical appearance.

When Looks
Can Kill

John Naish

> "*Women who undergo plastic surgery have a much higher risk of killing themselves.*"

In the following viewpoint, John Naish argues that cosmetic surgery can lead to harmful outcomes for patients. He contends that many patients become depressed after the surgery. The author cites research that shows women who undergo cosmetic surgery have a much higher risk of suicide. In addition to the risk of suicide, he contends that many patients experience post-traumatic stress after surgery. Naish is a reporter for the *Daily Mail*, a British tabloid newspaper.

AS YOU READ, CONSIDER THE FOLLOWING QUESTIONS:

1. According to the author, how much higher is the suicide rate for women who have had breast implants?
2. Naish states that how many patients developed post-traumatic stress after cosmetic surgery?
3. What percentage of patients do surgeons refer to psychologists, according to the author?

Laura Pillarella was hugely disappointed the first time she had plastic surgery. The naturally attractive, but insecure, young woman had hoped the procedures to remove the bags under her eyes and insert a chin implant would improve not only her looks, but also her life. They didn't.

John Naish, "When Looks Can Kill," *Daily Mail* (UK), Janurary 25, 2011. Copyright © 2011 by Daily Mail (UK). All rights reserved. Reproduced by permission.

'When the bandages came off, I was disappointed,' she says. 'I wasn't beautiful—just different. It wasn't enough.'

So Laura planned another operation . . . and then another. For the next decade she became trapped in a vicious cycle of surgery, dissatisfaction and more surgery.

Finally, after her 15th procedure, a plastic surgeon told her the real problem with her looks was that she had had excessive amounts of surgery. It was too much for Laura to bear.

After spending more than £40,000 trying to be beautiful, she seriously thought about taking her own life.

"How did the facelift go?"

"How did the facelift go?," cartoon by Andrew Toos, www.CartoonStock.com. Copyright © Andrew Toos. Reproduction rights obtainable from www.CartoonStock.com.

'I had my suicide all worked out. I was going to rent a room in a hotel, get some sleeping tablets and wash them down with red wine,' says the American personal trainer and author.

'I wasn't going to leave a suicide note. People would know why I'd killed myself. One look at my face said it all—I'd made myself look hideously ugly. My face was lop-sided, my nose was too skinny, my lips were distorted and my chin was crooked.'

Laura is typical of many cosmetic surgery patients who are left profoundly depressed by their appearance afterwards.

New research shows that behind the 'easy glamour' of nip'n'tuck lies a silent epidemic of disappointment, leading to a wave of suicides.

FAST FACT

According to *Psychology Today*, cosmetic surgery patients reported no significant changes to their self-esteem or depression symptoms following their procedures.

Women who undergo plastic surgery have a much higher risk of killing themselves, say experts in the journal *Current Psychiatry Reports*.

Their conclusions were based on five large-scale, independent studies, which found that the suicide rate is up to three times higher in women who have had breast implants.

The toll is not only restricted to suicides—cosmetic surgery patients had a three-times higher rate of death due to self-destructive acts, such as binge-drinking, drug overdoses and reckless driving.

Psychological damage related to plastic surgery is 'a critically neglected area', said researchers from the International Epidemiology Institute in the U.S.

Meanwhile, another study found that in eight out of ten cosmetic surgery practices, former patients had developed post-traumatic stress.

Surgeons were seeing at least as many psychological side effects as physical complications.

'Disappointment, anxiety and depression were the most frequently seen psychological problems,' says the report, published in the journal, *Plastic and Reconstructive Surgery*.

'The next frontier for the specialty is to improve patients' emotional and psychological results.'

It's a problem not just confined to women—indeed, men are thought more likely to be distraught at the outcome of their cosmetic surgery, even if they have had a 'technically good result', say researchers.

Last year, in journal *Annals of Plastic Surgery*, Melbourne University researchers advocated increased psychological screening before surgery and support for patients afterwards.

Such help was sadly never offered to Colin Phillips, 62. In 2009, an inquest in Cardiff heard how he hanged himself in a wood, distraught at how his third facelift had gone.

Phillips, a retired managing director, was 'fanatical' about his looks and had twice before undergone plastic surgery on his face.

But he felt his appearance had been butchered after a third procedure by a Harley Street surgeon and refused to leave his £600,000 home.

His wife, Janice, 62, said: 'After the first facelift he felt tremendous.'

But her husband's original surgeon refused to operate on him a third time, so he searched the internet for a Harley Street doctor who would.

The mother-of-two said: 'He was pinning his hopes on having a maxi-facelift. But after the operation he would look in the mirror shaking.'

A month later, Mr Phillips, a grandfather, took an overdose of drugs and was admitted to hospital. After being discharged, he made two other failed suicide attempts.

Finally, eight months after the operation, Mr Phillips killed himself.

As the demand for cosmetic surgery grows, such post-operative distress can only increase, say experts.

A study carried out for the Girl Guides recently found almost half of secondary school girls said they plan to have plastic surgery.

'Girls and young women tell us they are finding it hard to accept their appearance, and it is starting at a much earlier age than we had previously thought,' says Nicola Grinstead, of Girlguiding, UK.

Experts such as Professor Nichola Rumsey, a director of the UK Centre For Appearance Research, fear the underlying psychological issues that trigger the desire for plastic surgery are not being addressed.

People seeking cosmetic surgery often believe that it will solve dissatisfactions with their lives.

Laura Pillarella, the woman driven to plan suicide after 15 unsatisfactory procedures, said: 'I was manipulating my face to build a new self. I was lonely as a child. My parents split up when I was six. Mum would often say giving birth to me and my brothers had ruined her looks and body.

'I was distant from my dad and lacked emotional security so I was trying to boost my self-esteem. But plastic surgery never worked and each operation strengthened my quest to fix myself.'

Mercifully, her suicide plans stopped when her brother asked her to speak at his wedding. Suddenly, she says, she felt valued and began, slowly, to realise her unhappiness came from emotional problems.

Now aged 41, she has written a book charting her experiences, *Chasing Beauty: My Cosmetic Surgery Takeover*. 'If I had my time again,' she says, 'I wouldn't have surgery. I'd have therapy.'

One risk of cosmetic surgery is the patient's dissatisfaction with the end result. Many patients who feel the surgery did not enhance their appearance are left feeling depressed, which may lead to more procedures in an attempt to "fix" the problem.

It's a message that Charles Nduka, an NHS plastic surgeon, wishes many patients could hear.

'We are seeing a lot more people with psychological problems seeking plastic surgery,' says Nduka, who works at the Queen Victoria Hospital in East Grinstead, West Sussex.

There are two types of these patients, he says. Those who have pre-existing psychological issues with their appearance, such as body dysmorphic disorder, and should be having psychiatric help rather than surgery; and young women who are perfectly attractive, but have been made deeply unhappy with their bodies by constantly comparing themselves with airbrushed models.

'Often, these young women have a small amount of breast asymmetry, which causes them anxiety due to the "perfection" they see in magazines. But 90 per cent of women have a degree of asymmetry.'

Unrealistic expectations of surgical results are another growing problem, says Nduka.

'Ethical surgeons spend a lot of time talking to patients about their motivations for surgery and what they will achieve,' says Nduka, who runs the not-for-profit website safercosmeticsurgery.co.uk. He increasingly finds himself referring patients to psychologists.

Indeed, one survey found that surgeons refer about 20 per cent of patients to psychologists due to unrealistic expectations—they may believe it will improve their lives dramatically by getting them the glamorous job or the partner they want.

But Nduka warns that often patients never go to the psychologist and seek out a less scrupulous cosmetic surgeon.

Such patients can get caught in a costly and traumatic spiral of serial surgery, says Professor Rumsey.

'Vulnerable customers are initially pleased, but when the euphoria wears off, their disappointment with their looks returns. So they have another procedure.

'The problem is exacerbated by hard-sell incentives that are offered by some non-mainstream providers. Some even offer discounts for people who want more operations,' she says.

Nduka says many UK clinics do not follow good practice and is worried by the 'buy one get one free' (BOGOF) offers and aggressive marketing that 'plays on people's insecurity'.

'Often in these places, you meet a salesperson before a surgeon. One lady I saw went in for a consultation about eye wrinkles and the salesperson said: "Never mind your eyes, what about those wrinkles around your neck?"'

Three years ago, the British Association of Aesthetic Plastic Surgeons (BAAPS) launched a campaign to halt bad practice, such as bonus cards and BOGOF offers.

However, the association—which represents about a third of cosmetic surgeons—is not a regulatory body and has no powers to take action.

Mr Nduka wants to see health warnings on overseas treatment. 'Patients who end up going abroad only get one follow-up appointment. But they need more than this.'

This is also an issue in the UK, as doctors can set themselves up as plastic surgeons without being properly trained.

Nigel Mercer, president of BAAPS, says: 'In Britain you can call yourself something—such as a facial plastic surgeon—and need no relevant qualifications or training. In this respect, we are worse than anywhere else in Europe. Terrible things are happening to patients.'

BAAPS and the Care Quality Commission (the independent health care regulator) are drawing up Europe-wide standards of safe practice and regulation.

Mercer says: 'Patients ought to be able to get referrals to good clinical psychologists after the event if someone is having problems. It is very important.'

EVALUATING THE AUTHOR'S ARGUMENTS

In this viewpoint, John Naish claims that cosmetic surgery can have negative impacts on the mental health of patients. Do you find his argument more convincing than that of Katja Keuchenius, author of the following viewpoint? Why or why not?

Viewpoint

2

Cosmetic Surgery Boosts Self-Esteem

Katja Keuchenius

"Patients undergoing plastic surgery benefit psychologically."

In the following viewpoint, Katja Keuchenius interviews Jürgen Margraf, a German clinical and research psychologist whose studies show that plastic surgery can improve a patient's mental health. Prior to the study, the researcher spoke to several cosmetic surgeons who believed on average that their patients were happy with the outcome of surgery on a medical and psychological level. After the researcher concluded his study, he found that the results supported the viewpoint of the surgeons. He found that cosmetic surgery patients experience a psychological benefit from the outcome of the procedure and that this boost can last for up to a year. Keuchenius is an editor for *United Academics* magazine.

AS YOU READ, CONSIDER THE FOLLOWING QUESTIONS:

1. According to the journal *Clinical Psychological Science* cited by Keuchenius, how long does the psychological improvement from plastic surgery generally last?
2. Which would be easier to assess, according to Margraf, happiness or satisfaction and self-assurance?
3. What is the average level of goal attainment for cosmetic surgery patients, according to Margraf?

Katja Keuchenius, "Plastic Surgery Improves Mental Health," *United Academics*, June 27, 2013. Copyright © 2013 by United Academics. All rights reserved. Reproduced by permission.

The journal *Clinical Psychological Science* recently [March 4, 2013] published an article stating that patients undergoing plastic surgery benefit psychologically from the physical changes, with the improvement lasting at least a year.

But at the bottom of the research report there was a disturbing sentence. It said that the study was funded by Mang Medical One AG, a large provider of plastic surgery in Germany. So can we really trust the optimistic conclusion about the effects of cosmetic operations? Prof. Dr. Jürgen Margraf, leader of the study, answers some questions:

[Katja Keuchenius:] Who came up with the idea for this study?

[Jürgen Margraf:] The funder contacted me for scientific advice. They had the impression that their patients were on average quite happy with the outcome of surgery, on a medical *and* psychological level. They also thought that their patients became more self-assured. Yet, in the general discussion, especially in Germany, aesthetic surgery in their opinion was totally misrepresented. So they wanted to show that many patients would "be much happier" after surgery.

FAST FACT

With fifty-two procedures at a total cost of $100,000 as of 2012, Cindy Jackson holds the record for the most cosmetic surgery, according to *Guinness World Records*.

You ended up conducting the study, how did you protect your independence?

I told them that "happiness" as an outcome would be difficult, but that satisfaction and self-assurance could be assessed reliably, if we would be a totally independent research team. We asked for a control group and for a representative comparison group from the general population, although this made the study much more expensive. The subjects had already been operated at one of the clinics of Mang Medical One AG. We were ensured that we would only be presented with consecutive cases with only the inclusion/exclusion criteria we set up. We analyzed the data, checked plausibility and were able to collect the reasons for people not participating. We had the right to

Patient Ratings for Top Cosmetic Procedures, 2013

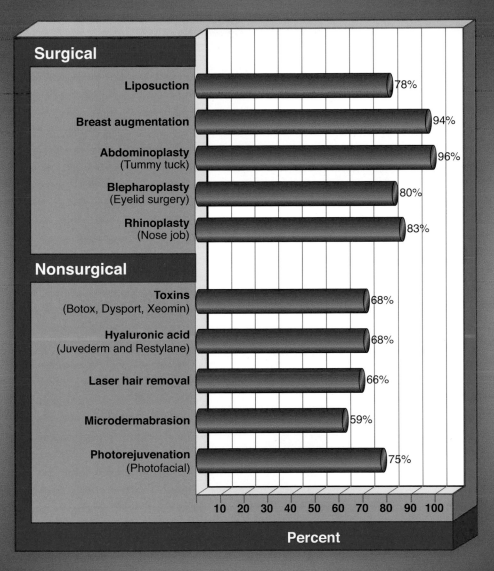

Surgical

Liposuction	78%
Breast augmentation	94%
Abdominoplasty (Tummy tuck)	96%
Blepharoplasty (Eyelid surgery)	80%
Rhinoplasty (Nose job)	83%

Nonsurgical

Toxins (Botox, Dysport, Xeomin)	68%
Hyaluronic acid (Juvederm and Restylane)	68%
Laser hair removal	66%
Microdermabrasion	59%
Photorejuvenation (Photofacial)	75%

10 20 30 40 50 60 70 80 90 100

Percent

Data from the "RealSelf Worth-It Rating" for the American Society for Aesthetic Plastic Surgery. The ratings reflect the combined opinions of thousands of RealSelf.com community members. Members shared whether an elective surgery or treatment was "worth it" all things considered. Worth-It Ratings are expressed as a percentage; for example, an 80% Worth-It rating means 8 out of 10 patients would do it again.

Taken from: Cosmetic Surgery National Data Bank Statistics, "RealSelf Worth-It Ratings for ASAPS Top 5 Surgical and Nonsurgical Procedures—2013," American Society for Aesthetic Plastic Surgery, 2013.

Some evidence suggests that cosmetic surgery patients are happy with their results and continue to receive a psychological boost to their self-esteem.

publish the results and were in no way influenced (in fact not even contacted) during the article's writing process.

You made use of a control group of participants who changed their minds about having plastic surgery. How did you find these people?

The control group was a very difficult part of the study. The scientifically best solution (i.e., random assignment to surgery or no surgery) was not possible for both ethical and practical reasons. We thus came up with the idea of looking at people who had shown interest in surgery but had not yet decided about it. These were recruited from people who had contacted the provider's website, but had not made an appointment. We were able to recruit some 250 for the study and asked them why. The most frequent answer was financial reasons, if I recall right. The control group members typically were still thinking about an operation, at least as far as we knew.

What were your expectations?

I was personally surprised by several of our findings. I had expected to find more subjects with unrealistic goals, a greater share of subjects with clinically relevant anxiety/depression and a lower level of goal attainment. And—most of all—I suspected the improvement of psychological well-being of the subjects (including self-esteem, quality of life and mental health) to return to pre-intervention levels.

A large body of evidence shows that people go back to initial levels rather quickly, even after major life events (both positive and negative, see for instance Ed Diener's work). We tested the patients up to a year after surgery. It is possible that we will see differences during a longer follow-up, but typically you should see at least the beginning of this during the first year.

So you state that "embodied changes via aesthetic surgery may produce more permanent psychological change than more temporary or malleable life events, such as relationship changes, relocations, and so on." Isn't that a bit too enthusiastic?

I don't think it is enthusiastic and I am not sure what I would recommend to any given individual. In my clinical practice, I normally see people with mental disorders and for them I have not recommended aesthetic surgery. But, as our study showed, most people undergoing aesthetic surgery do not come with mental disorders and do not think that surgery will alleviate such disorders. Instead, they come with a circumscribed aesthetic problem and want exactly this to be changed (e.g., nose correction, but not a total change of the face or the personality). Our data show that that is what they get, with an average level of some 80% goal attainment. Embodiment is a particularly interesting candidate for possible explanation. This will require further studies, however.

EVALUATING THE AUTHOR'S ARGUMENTS

In this viewpoint, Jürgen Margraf—as interviewed by Katja Keuchenius—claims that cosmetic surgery can have a positive psychological impact on patients. Who has a more convincing argument, Margraf or John Naish, the author of the preceding viewpoint? Explain.

The "Selfie" Trend Increases Demand for Plastic Surgery

American Academy of Facial Plastic and Reconstructive Surgery

"Patients [are] more self-aware of looks in social media."

In the following viewpoint, the American Academy of Facial Plastic and Reconstructive Surgery (AAFPRS) contends that the rise of photo sharing on social media sites is linked to an increase in the number of patients undergoing facial cosmetic surgery procedures. Social media have a powerful influence on youth, the author contends, and research shows an increase in cosmetic procedures in patients under thirty years old. The AAFPRS is the world's largest association of facial plastic surgery professionals.

AS YOU READ, CONSIDER THE FOLLOWING QUESTIONS:

1. According to the author, what percentage of AAFPRS members identified a link between social media usage and an increase in patients seeking cosmetic surgery?
2. The AAFPRS states that what percentage of youth are undergoing cosmetic surgery because of bullying?

"Annual AAFPRS Survey Finds 'Selfie' Trend Increases Demand for Facial Plastic Surgery Influence on Elective Surgery," American Academy of Facial Plastic and Reconstructive Surgery, March 11, 2014. aafprs .org. Copyright © 2014 by American Academy of Facial Plastic and Reconstructive. All rights reserved. Reproduced by permission.

The rise of 'selfies' is having a huge impact on the facial plastic surgery industry according to a new [March 2014] study by the American Academy of Facial Plastic and Reconstructive Surgery (AAFPRS). The annual poll studies a select group of the organization's 2,700 members to uncover the latest trends in facial plastic surgery.

The study revealed that one in three facial plastic surgeons surveyed saw an increase in requests for procedures due to patients being more self-aware of looks in social media. In fact, 13 percent of AAFPRS members surveyed identified increased photo sharing and patients' dissatisfaction with their own image on social media sites as a rising trend in practice. As a result, AAFPRS members surveyed noted a 10 percent increase in rhinoplasty in 2013 over 2012, as well as a 7 percent increase in hair transplants and a 6 percent increase in eyelid surgery.

"Social platforms like Instagram, Snapchat and the iPhone app Selfie.im, which are solely image based, force patients to hold a microscope up to their own image and often look at it with a more self-critical eye than ever before," says Edward Farrior, MD, President of

Some plastic surgeons believe the "selfie" trend has led to an increase in cosmetic surgery procedures as people strive to look as good as possible on social media.

the American Academy of Facial Plastic and Reconstructive Surgery. "These images are often the first impressions young people put out there to prospective friends, romantic interests and employers and our patients want to put their best face forward."

Bullying is also a factor, but most surgeons surveyed report children and teens are undergoing plastic surgery as a result of being bullied (69 percent) rather than to prevent being bullied (31 percent).

> ## FAST FACT
>
> The American Society for Aesthetic Plastic Surgery reported that the number of cosmetic procedures in the United States jumped from 2.1 million to 10 million from 1997 to 2012.

The Face of Plastic Surgery Gets Younger

There's no denying that social media plays a particularly influential role in teens' lives and self-esteem, so it's no surprise that it's also a driving force behind an increasingly youthful face of plastic surgery. In 2013, more than half of surveyed facial plastic surgeons (58 percent) saw an increase in cosmetic surgery or injectables in those under age 30.

Both men and women are becoming increasingly aware of the aging process, and of what can be done to turn back the clock. The AAFPRS survey found that 39 percent of members surveyed stated there is a rise in the demand for non-surgical cosmetic procedures to delay facial surgery. Thirty-four percent of facial surgeons surveyed stated that women under 35 are looking after their skin to prevent visible signs of aging for longer, while 23 percent of facial surgeons surveyed stated that men under 35 are seeking rhinoplasty, neck liposuction, chin implants, and acne scar reduction procedures.

"The top five things most patients are most concerned with are results, cost, recovery, pain and scars," says Dr. Farrior. "Whether driven by a desire to stay competitive in the workforce, remain attractive to their mate or simply to look as good as they feel, advances in non-invasive anti-aging technologies are making it possible to delay the hands of time while retaining a natural outcome. As recovery times are reduced and results are more subtle, aesthetic procedures become a more viable maintenance option for young men and women."

Increase in Plastic Surgery Requests Due to Social Media Use

Have you seen an increase in requests for plastic surgery stemming from people being more self-aware of their looks because of social media? If so, estimate the percentage of requests for each procedure.

	2012	2013
Any requests	31%	33%
Rhinoplasty (nose)	22%	28%
Botox	19%	20%
Face-lifts	17%	16%
Blepharoplasty (eyelids)	16%	13%
Chin augmentation	12%	13%
Lip augmentation	10%	4%
Otoplasty (ears)	7%	9%
Facial implants	NA	1%
Forehead lift	5%	4%
Scar revision	5%	4%
Hair transplantation	3%	3%
Eyebrow transplants	2%	0%

Note: N for 2012 = 58; N for 2013 = 69. Data collected by the American Academy of Facial Plastic and Reconstructive Surgery (AAFPRS) via a web survey of AAFPRS members between January 18 and February 5, 2014.

Taken from: International Communications Research, "2013 AAFPRS Membership Study," February 2014. www.aafprs.org.

Almost three quarters of all procedures performed in 2013 were minimally invasive. Of these, BOTOX® Cosmetic made up approximately half of all minimally invasive procedures performed, followed by hyaluronic acid and peels.

Cosmetic Procedures Differ Between Men and Women

Women continue to be the most likely candidates for facial plastic surgery and account for 81 percent of all surgical and non-surgical procedures in 2013. In fact, mothers are the most likely candidates, making up two-thirds of all procedures on women last year.

Men are most concerned with wrinkles and having a full head of hair, while women value preserving their youthful appearance with a facelift and eye lift as well as having a well-proportioned, attractive nose.

Among male patients, the most popular procedures were BOTOX®, hyaluronic acid injections, hair transplants and rhinoplasty.

The most common cosmetic surgical procedures performed on women were facelifts and rhinoplasties (average of 37 procedures per surgeon each), ablative skin resurfacing (36 procedures) and blepharoplasty (34 procedures). In 2013, BOTOX®, still reigned supreme as the most commonly performed non-surgical procedure among women (348 procedures), followed by hyaluronic acid injections (187 procedures), superficial peels/microdermabrasion (119 procedures), and non-ablative resurfacing (106 procedures).

Meanwhile, "rhinopopularity" still dominates both sexes, with nose jobs being the most requested surgical procedure for both men and women under the age of 35 (90 percent and 86 percent, respectively).

Families Are Getting Surgery Together

Familial bonding through plastic surgery is on the rise, with the survey revealing an 8 percent increase in female family members undergoing procedures together. Husbands and wives are actually the most likely to opt for having cosmetic surgery together, with 31 percent of facial surgeons surveyed indicating an increase in married plastic surgery requests in 2013. Women tend to be the driving force behind the decision, however, with 21 percent of male plastic surgery requests resulting from their significant other having undergone facial plastic surgery.

Consumers Are Becoming More Savvy

Thanks to the wealth of information available to patients on the Internet, consumers become more and more savvy about choosing a surgeon each year. Forty-four percent of AAFPRS members surveyed noticed their patients being more educated about plastic surgery than ever before. Most patients got their information about plastic surgery online (60 percent), followed by referrals from friends (53 percent).

Consumers' deepening knowledge of the field is indicated by how patients ask for procedures. Rather than asking for a feature by celebrity reference, as was a trend in year's past, more than half of patients (59 percent) now ask for procedures by describing the area of concern (nasal hump, crow's feet, sagging neck), whereas one quarter (26 percent) ask for the surgeon's advice.

While the Internet is an excellent tool for researching surgeons and procedural information, the AAFPRS urges consumers to beware of "too good to be true" discounted deals on procedures.

"Our members nearly unanimously agree that prospective patients need to exercise caution when considering an online deal," says Dr. Farrior. "To ensure the best results, you should have a consultation with your prospective physician to assess your candidacy and clearly discuss your goals. Always make sure to select a board-certified surgeon who specializes in plastic surgery of the face, head and neck."

EVALUATING THE AUTHOR'S ARGUMENTS

In this viewpoint, the American Academy of Facial Plastic and Reconstructive Surgery claims that the "selfie" trend on social media has led to a rise in patients undergoing cosmetic surgery. Do you think the author's contention of a link between social media and a rise in cosmetic surgery patients is valid? Why or why not?

Viewpoint

4

Cosmetic Surgery Should Not Be Judged Morally

"People do what they need to do. How does it help to criticize them?"

Jane Ganahl

In the following viewpoint, Jane Ganahl maintains that plastic surgery does not hinder one's spiritual growth. The author examines the phenomenon of plastic surgery through the lens of spiritual exploration and shares six lessons that she has learned from her research. The key for those on a spiritual path, the author maintains, is to embrace the authentic self and cultivate inner happiness. For some, Ganahl contends, that path may include a tummy tuck or a face lift. Ganahl is the author of *Naked on the Page* and the editor of the anthology *Single Woman of a Certain Age*.

AS YOU READ, CONSIDER THE FOLLOWING QUESTIONS:

1. According to the author, what is the most popular cosmetic surgery procedure in the United States?
2. How does Isabella Rossellini refer to cosmetic surgery, as stated by the author?
3. What is the largest demographic of those who get face-lifts, according to Ganahl?

Jane Ganahl, "The Plastic Surgery Debate: Spiritual Exploration in the Age of Cosmetic Surgery," *Utne Reader*, November–December 2013. Copyright © 2013 by Jane Ganahl. All rights reserved. Reproduced by permission.

Only a few decades ago, plastic surgery was limited to socialites and other women with money and a big stake in looking perpetually 25. Now it's positively mainstream. Even in enlightened circles—at yoga and meditation classes, and at ashrams [Hindu spiritual centers] and Buddhist temples—you can see the strangely tight faces, the too-pouty lips, the breasts that defy gravity. If plastic surgery has confounded me in general, the indulgence in it by those following a spiritual path—a path that emphasizes transcendence of the ego—leaves me flummoxed.

No fewer than 14.6 million cosmetic plastic surgery procedures—both minimally invasive and surgical—were performed in this country in 2012. In order of popularity: breast augmentations, nose jobs, liposuctions, eyelid surgeries, face-lifts, and tummy tucks.

FAST FACT

According to the American Society for Aesthetic Plastic Surgery, 67 percent of Americans would not find it embarrassing if their friends or family knew about their cosmetic surgery.

Yet some indicators hint that a backlash has begun. In Hollywood, Isabella Rossellini has referred to cosmetic surgery as "the new foot binding";[1] Salma Hayek blasted it as "the uniform of a generation"; Halle Berry calls its proliferation "really insane, and I feel sad that that's what society is doing to women." And Emma Thompson, Rachel Weisz, and Kate Winslet have formed what they have dubbed the "British Anti-Plastic Surgery League."

Other signposts are popping up. Sixtyish model Cindy Joseph has created a cosmetics line, Boom, aimed at women of a certain age, and business is (ahem) booming.

"I feel like we've reached a tipping point, and women are waking up," she says. "It's exciting to see how many women are beginning to see the beauty of aging and wearing it with style. We love our wrinkles and wear them proudly.". . .

All of these thoughts on the controversy set me on a path to examine the phenomenon of plastic surgery through a lens of spiritual exploration. In the course of my journey, I've learned six key lessons from the Great Plastic Surgery Debate.

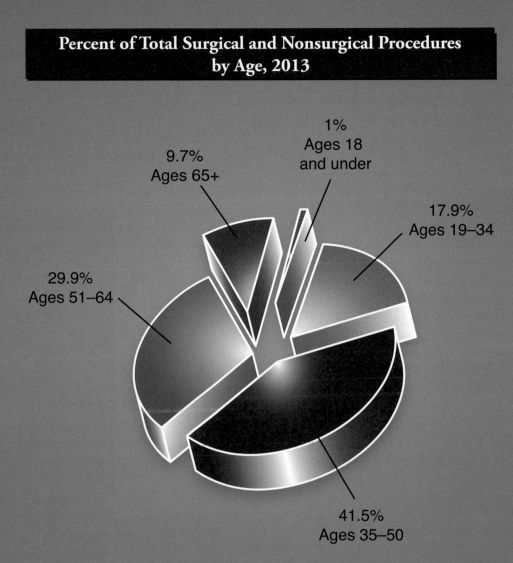

Percent of Total Surgical and Nonsurgical Procedures by Age, 2013

1%
Ages 18 and under

9.7%
Ages 65+

17.9%
Ages 19–34

29.9%
Ages 51–64

41.5%
Ages 35–50

Taken from: Cosmetic Surgery National Data Bank Statistics, "2013 Age Distribution for Cosmetic Procedures," American Society for Aesthetic Plastic Surgery, 2013.

Lesson 1: We Avoid the Present Moment

From hormone replacement pills to Viagra to yoga poses that promise better skin, it has never been easier to avoid the signs of aging. But that raises the question: why should we want to? . . .

I know that in my own life, aging has offered me some fantastic benefits: from excellent friendships to time to read, from a greater understanding of the human heart to an appreciation of Shakespeare. But savoring those things requires slowing down life's frantic pace and embracing the present moment, seeing the beauty of the age I am, rather than pining for a younger version of me.

The media theorist Douglas Rushkoff, author of *Present Shock*, makes the argument that our culture is stuck in what he calls "the short forever."

"Fighting time is not only impossible but counterproductive," he says. "When people try to freeze time, they lose access to the living moment." . . .

Lesson 2: We Can't Deal with Impermanence

"This is definitely a youth-obsessed culture," says the Buddhist teacher Lewis Richmond, author of *Aging as a Spiritual Practice*. "It's almost impossible for us to grasp the idea that nothing is permanent and everything is in flux, including our identity and including us." . . .

Yet accepting that impermanence can also bring great joy. "The evanescence of things is the reason you enjoy your life," he says. "A plastic flower might look pretty on first glance and will be around forever, but only a real flower, which will wilt and drop its leaves soon after blossoming, is truly beautiful."

How does this relate to women who strive to never change? "When you cling to what you know you will lose, you suffer needlessly," Richmond says. "But embracing impermanence is opening the door to joy."

Lesson 3: Older Women Feel Invisible

Not surprisingly, the largest demographic getting face-lifts comprises women pushing 50.

"Men buy Ferraris; women buy face-lifts, because they want to feel that they are still wanted, valued, and desirable," says Lynn Forbes, cofounder of the Whoa Network, an online community for women at midlife and beyond. "Women feel less powerful, less seen and heard as they age." Old is deemed bad and young is good in our culture, says Forbes, which is why so many women this age suffer from a lack of self-esteem. . . .

For Carole Simone, a Northern California spiritual coach and healer, women's reasons for seeking a nip or tuck all boil down to one thing: "I see clients all day long who are having procedures done, and they're confused about it," she says. "They're concerned about how lovable they are. I don't have any judgments about [surgery], but if I can help them see themselves as strong and beautiful, then they can make a solid decision about it. But I have compassion for any woman who questions whether she is worthy of love, as should we all.". . .

Lesson 4: We Judge Others and Are Judged

[My friend] Wendy is philosophical. "I think it's just human nature to judge—but the judger might want to pause and reflect on what it is they have contempt for, and why." As I wrote once, 'Whatever I have contempt for, I might just as well set a place for it at my table, because it is either in my life already, or coming.'"

Simone agrees. "Judgment is all about fear, and under fear there is a lot of projection. You may think you know someone well, but you don't know their deepest story. People have to find that place inside themselves that is big and inclusive."

Richmond, the Buddhist teacher, evolved in his perspective toward cosmetic surgery after hearing poignant personal stories from women. "Ageism threatens their livelihood and their sense of who they are. People do what they need to do. How does it help to criticize them?"

Lesson 5: We Need to Know What We're Getting Into

In addition to the potential for emotional and spiritual side effects, cosmetic procedures do carry some health risks—from the (fortunately rare) horror stories of badly botched surgeries, to more common complications that can lead to a difficult recovery or long-term pain. . . .

If you're contemplating taking this step yourself, Simone suggests a meditative exercise. "I encourage anyone considering this to go inside themselves and ask one question of the wise-woman part of them. Ask that wise woman, 'What are you trying to tell me?' And listen to that. And then ask the wise woman if this is the highest good."

She advocates a thoughtful, cautious approach. "When you quiet down and get away from your fear, ask yourself, 'What are you afraid of?' And if you can work with that part that is afraid, then you can make a good decision. I just always try to remind people that you can always be more beautiful, but it won't bring more joy into your life.". . .

Lesson 6: Everyone Can Win

Embrace your authentic self—whether that means getting that boob job or celebrating your crow's-feet and gray mane. See what makes you happy in this bold experiment called life. And proceed with caution and think things through before getting a dragon tattoo or face-lift.

Reconsider the concept of beauty. "We need to change the whole notion of what true beauty is," says Joseph. "When a woman feels good in her skin, when she's happy and joyful and finds her true purpose and passions, she shines from the inside out."

Cultivate inner happiness by giving of yourself. Volunteer at a senior center, organize a book club, audition for community theater. Doing for others keeps you from obsessing about those crow's-feet.

Buck the cultural impediments to visibility. Walk tall, refuse to take a table by the kitchen [in a restaurant], make your opinions known. Change the way you look at yourself, and the world will change too.

Turn over a new leaf. "Reinvention is huge for women at this age," says Forbes. "They call it the f—k-you 50s for a reason. We're finally at a point where we have the courage to be ourselves, do what we want, surround ourselves with the people we want to be with. I find this time amazing.

"But," she adds, laughing, "I still don't like the crow's-feet."

Note

1. Foot binding was an ancient Chinese practice of tightly wrapping a young girl's feet to restrict their growth. It was considered a mark of beauty and a status symbol, but was later viewed as demeaning to women.

EVALUATING THE AUTHOR'S ARGUMENTS

In this viewpoint, Jane Ganahl maintains that cosmetic surgery does not compromise one's spirituality. On the basis of her arguments, do you think she would agree with Richard J. Poupard, author of the following viewpoint, about the ethics of cosmetic surgery? Why or why not?

Cosmetic Surgery Should Be Judged Morally and Ethically

Richard J. Poupard

"I can find no reason to find cosmetic surgery intrinsically immoral."

In the following viewpoint, Richard J. Poupard examines the ethical implications of plastic surgery. He maintains that cosmetic surgery should not be condemned outright from a religious perspective; however, he believes that the motivation behind getting such surgery determines the ethics of the decision. He believes that consumers should consider whether their goal is to normalize their appearance or to enhance their bodies to more closely approach some ideal. It is impossible to achieve the ideal by undergoing cosmetic surgery, the author argues, and the only way to satisfy the longing for perfection is to find true happiness from the inside out. Poupard is a board-certified oral and maxillofacial surgeon in Midland, Michigan. He is also a speaker for Life Training Institute, a nonprofit seminary that focuses on ministry, wellness, and recovery from a biblical perspective.

Richard J. Poupard, "Self-Esteem from a Scalpel: The Ethics of Plastic Surgery," *Christian Research Journal*, vol. 33, no. 4, 2013. Copyright © 2013 by Christian Research Journal. All rights reserved. Reproduced by permission.

AS YOU READ, CONSIDER THE FOLLOWING QUESTIONS:
1. Plastic surgery is divided into what two categories, according to the author?
2. According to Poupard, what is the main purpose of medical science?
3. What is the goal of reconstructive surgery, as stated by the author?

The numbers of patients seeking plastic surgery has skyrocketed in the past decade, and this practice has found increasingly uncritical acceptance. Plastic surgery is commonly subdivided into reconstructive surgery and cosmetic surgery. Reconstructive surgery seeks to restore form and function of a defect in the body, and therefore is a positive moral good that mitigates the effects of the fall [of humankind into a sinful state]. Cosmetic surgery differs in that we are seeking to augment otherwise healthy tissues to improve appearance and self-esteem. . . . I do not believe we have license to condemn all forms of cosmetic surgery. We should be discerning,

"Of course, there's a *possibility* that you are a swan,
but do you want to take that risk?"

"Cosmetic surgeon tells Ugly Duckling: 'Of course, there's a POSSIBILITY that you are a swan, but do you want to take that risk?'," cartoon by Royston Robertson, www.CartoonStock.com. Copyright © Royston Robertson. Reproduction rights obtainable from www.CartoonStock.com.

however, regarding our motivations for pursuing cosmetic surgery. First, we should be careful if our motivations for surgery are principally to increase our self-esteem. The evidence shows the long-term effects of cosmetic surgery are not universally positive, and we should be esteemed not based on our own image, but the image of the God who created us and died for us. Second, we should consider whether our goal for surgery is to normalize our appearance or to enhance our bodies to approximate a perfect ideal. If cosmetic perfection to increase the attention others give us is our motivation, we may not be adhering to the principle of biblical modesty. Last, surgical enhancement supports the idea that our bodies are ours to modify without limit. . . .

The Ethics of Cosmetic Surgery

The main purpose of medical science is to treat sickness and disease, thus helping to alleviate suffering. This is not only the case for surgery, but for all other types of medical treatment. Reconstructive surgery is simply the application of this principle when there is a pathological, congenital, or traumatic defect. Since the goal in reconstructive surgery is to restore form and function to damaged tissue, this type of surgery is a moral good. . . .

> **FAST FACT**
>
> According to *The Guardian*, an unusual type of plastic surgery is the voice lift, a complex procedure on the vocal folds to make the patient's voice sound younger or fuller.

Cosmetic surgery differs because there is not a restoration of pathologic tissue, but an augmentation of healthy tissue. There historically has been controversy regarding cosmetic surgery because it was seen to corrupt the natural body-self relation. This argument, however, as well as the stigma behind cosmetic surgery procedures, has largely faded from our culture. Does the fact that we are operating on otherwise healthy tissue make cosmetic surgeries unethical in all circumstances? I believe there are a number of reasons why we should not make this blanket condemnation. . . .

I can find no reason to find cosmetic surgery intrinsically immoral. Yet, although a specific action may not be intrinsically immoral or scripturally prohibited does not mean that it is profitable in every circumstance. We may be tempted, due to our sinful hearts, to engage in an activity for immoral goals or reasons. Our motivations for pursuing cosmetic surgery have an important impact on the ethics of the act itself. For this reason, there are some important caveats to consider when discerning the ethics of cosmetic surgery. . . .

Examining the Role of Self-Image

There is no doubt that many consider themselves unattractive, either based on a disfiguring pathology or simply because they don't "fit in" in our beauty-obsessed culture. Surgically changing the outward form of their bodies may in many cases increase self-esteem, at least for a time. There is no question that we can get an emotional lift when we believe we feel attractive on a particular day. The difficulties begin, however, when we become dependent on that emotional lift from our own attractiveness as essential to our value. Furthermore, when

A photo illustration shows before-and-after images of skin care options. Some feel it is unethical to undergo plastic surgery if the motivation is only the attainment of a "perfect" look.

parents convince their children that cosmetic surgery is necessary for their self-esteem, the unavoidable message is that we are valued based predominantly on our outward appearance.

This is not to say that there is anything wrong with a desire to be attractive. Being a good steward of the body given to us is a positive good. There is nothing wrong with taking a glance in the mirror when wearing a particularly attractive dress or feeling satisfied with the results of a month-long workout program. I don't believe there is any virtue in intentionally allowing ourselves to become unattractive, or in highlighting a particularly unattractive aspect of our physical self. The problem ensues when we value ourselves predominantly on the image that we see as we look into that mirror. If our motivation for undergoing a permanent surgical change is to increase the value we have in our own eyes when we peer at our image, then we are looking at the wrong image for our esteem. It is not our image that gives us value, but the God in whose image we were created. Regardless of how we look on the outside, this should not be forgotten. . . .

Analyzing the Ethics of Cosmetic Surgery

It may be helpful to differentiate between two types of cosmetic surgery. A procedure such as the removal of a visible, unaesthetic birthmark is attempting to change a physical "abnormality" into a more normal situation. On the other hand, someone returning multiple times to multiple surgeons to get their nose "just right" is attempting to *enhance* their normal anatomy to some perfect ideal. We can visualize this by looking at a continuum with the concept of "normal" at the center, and "abnormal" and "perfect" at the extremes. Some patients believe they are on the "abnormal" side of the continuum and their goal for their surgery is to look "normal" for the first time in their lives. The goals of other patients are to enhance their normal-looking bodies in an effort to approximate perfection. The ethics of these individual motivations may differ.

There are nuances to this evaluation. An obvious one is who decides the characteristics that make us "normal"? If normal is culturally determined, the greater numbers of individuals having cosmetic surgery is moving the standard. The standard of "pretty" was always somewhat pliable, but now we have to contend with the greater number of surgically enhanced bodies to change that standard even more. Regardless, there seems to be delineation between those who seek cosmetic surgery to not draw attention to their appearance, and those undergoing cosmetic surgery for the reason to draw more attention to their appearance. Motivations for cosmetic surgery that go beyond "normalizing" one's appearance are problematic. . . .

Normalization or Superhuman Enhancement?

There is an ongoing debate in bioethics concerning the idea of human enhancement. The rapid development and popularity of enhancement cosmetic surgery is being used as a template to analyze how we may choose to augment our bodies in other ways in the future. Mary Devereaux states, "Cosmetic surgery thus provides a natural starting point for an investigation of the likely future of medical enhancement." If this is the case, then the future of medical enhancement will be based solely on our subjective standards of what we desire or what will makes us happy; at least until we need another enhancement to bring us closer to our idealized standard of perfection. Medical professionals may cease to exist to cure disease. They will instead use their knowledge and skills to make us more enhanced. . . .

We will never find the perfect ideal from a surgeon's scalpel or needle. The short-lived boost of happiness that we may receive from having our faces or bodies surgically augmented does not have the ability to satisfy the great longing for perfection that exists in our hearts. The only possible way to true happiness and perfection is to grow in conformity to the image of Christ, the Creator of all beauty and life.

EVALUATING THE AUTHOR'S ARGUMENTS

In this viewpoint, Richard J. Poupard claims that cosmetic surgery can compromise one's spirituality. Whose argument is more convincing, his or Jane Ganahl's, the author of the preceding viewpoint? Explain your answer.

Cosmetic Surgery Should Not Be Condemned by Feminists

Angela Neustatter

"To me, the huge value of feminism has been . . . women supporting each other in their choices."

In the following viewpoint, Angela Neustatter argues that feminists should not condemn cosmetic surgery. The author relates her feelings of shame after undergoing a cosmetic procedure. She believes that feminists need to be more open-minded about cosmetic surgery and not equate the practice with body loathing. Society needs to tackle the objectification and self-esteem issues that afflict young women, the author argues, but ostracizing women who undergo plastic surgery from the feminist movement is not the answer. Neustatter is a journalist and the author of *A Home for the Heart* and *The Year I Turn . . . A Quirky A–Z of Ageing*.

AS YOU READ, CONSIDER THE FOLLOWING QUESTIONS:

1. According to the author, by what percentage have cosmetic surgery procedures risen since 2012?

Angela Neustatter, "I'm a Feminist and I've Had Cosmetic Surgery. Why Is That a Problem?," *The Guardian* (UK), February 3, 2014. Copyright Guardian News & Media Ltd., 2014. Reproduced by permission.

2. How many women had breast enhancement operations in 2013, as stated by Neustatter?
3. According to Neustatter, what is the value of feminism?

The memory of actor Julie Christie being accused, in print, of "betraying us all" when she admitted to having had a face lift to try to stay working in the mercilessly youth-adoring Hollywood culture, came sharply into focus as I read that cosmetic surgery procedures have risen by 17% on average since 2012.

I had an eye job in my 40s when my eyes seemed to be disappearing into a reptilian layer of skin folds. This made me miserable because we

Female Facial Plastic Surgery Patients

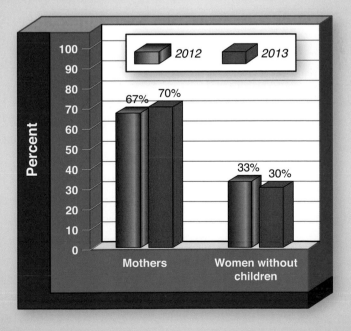

More than two thirds of female patients undergoing facial plastic surgery are mothers.

Taken from: International Communications Research, "2013 AAFPRS Membership Study," February 2014. www.aafprs.org.

communicate so much with our eyes, and journalists, more than most. I wrote about my eyelid surgery partly because so many feminists were tight-lipped about the procedures they had (and believe me, they did) and I felt it important to be honest about the way I, as a feminist, deal with the human condition. I hadn't anticipated the personal criticism and condemnation—I was accused of body loathing—that came my way. Feminists were not supposed to reveal such feminine frailty in the face of ageing it seemed.

Societal Pressures Encourage Cosmetic Procedures

I hope we can take a more nuanced approach now. If only because attack mode and high-mindedness have manifestly failed to put people off seeking surgery. Ever more and younger women are signing up for procedures, from breast enlargement to liposuction, which involves removing fat from areas of the body. According to statistics released this week, the number of liposuction procedures increased by more than 40% last year [2013] compared with 2012.

It is, of course, a tragic reflection of the values that have flooded our society so powerfully that we cannot just scoff at the glossy unreality of so much of the imagery that bombards us. Young people in particular cannot feel carefree about their appearance, which is why eating disorders, body dysmorphia and self-harm are all on the increase.

FAST FACT

Repeat customers made up about half of all cosmetic surgery patients in 2012, according to the American Society of Plastic Surgeons.

But those who choose the scalpel route are doing so to compete in a culture where youthful beauty is beamed at us as the most desirable thing there is. Despite the despair and sense of failure this message brings to many of us, research confirms that attractiveness brings more opportunities in both the work and romance departments. No wonder women, and increasingly men, frightened witless at the prospect of losing the clout which having visibly appealing looks brings, are heading for nips, tucks, lifts, botox and more. Despite the breast implants scandal [in which a French implant manufacturer used industrial-grade silicone instead of medical-grade silicone], 11,000 women had breast enhancement operations in 2013, an increase of 13% on the previous year.

Condemning Personal Choices Is Counterproductive

I am absolutely of the view that, as a society, we have much to do to tackle the objectification and self-esteem issues that afflict young women in particular. But I think we have to do it through dialogue and discussion with young women (and young men) who are ever-more prone to the looks culture. We have to make time to involve ourselves with them and help them to see the ways many of us have built rewarding lives without being drop-dead gorgeous. Indeed, the subject of my new book is the ways in which, as we mature, it can become easier to live with who and what we are.

The [UK] minister for women and equalities, Jo Swinson, has the right idea with the Campaign for Body Confidence she instigated and which has been taken up by the government. She talks of the need to open up the debate and talk more openly about how low body confidence at all ages affects performance in the workplace and family relationships.

Condemning individuals for decisions they take to compete in a culture they themselves didn't create is counterproductive and harmful, even if those decisions are ones we regard as medically unnecessary and politically distasteful. To me, the huge value of feminism has been the life-affirming value of women supporting each other in their choices. It is about understanding more, condemning less.

EVALUATING THE AUTHOR'S ARGUMENTS

In this viewpoint, Angela Neustatter claims that feminists should not condemn women for having plastic surgery. What is the argument for the opposing view that having cosmetic surgery compromises a woman's ability to be a feminist?

Chapter 3

Is Cosmetic Surgery for Everyone?

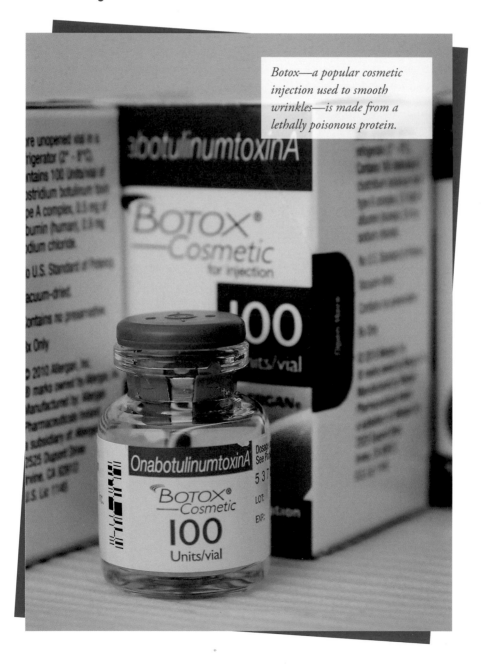

Botox—a popular cosmetic injection used to smooth wrinkles—is made from a lethally poisonous protein.

Can Plastic Surgery Be Good for Teens?

"Plastic surgery [for teens] can be altogether positive in the right circumstances."

Laura T. Coffey

In the following viewpoint, Laura T. Coffey explores the rising number of teenagers undergoing cosmetic surgery. The author reports that while adults undergo plastic surgery to stand out, many teens desire plastic surgery to fit in. While teens should take precautionary steps before going under the knife, in the right circumstances, the author finds that cosmetic surgery can be beneficial for teens. It can correct a physical defect that may have caused the teen psychological distress and offer a boost of self-confidence. Coffey is a writer, editor, and producer for Today.com.

AS YOU READ, CONSIDER THE FOLLOWING QUESTIONS:

1. According to the author, what is the number of therapy sessions recommended for teen patients before undergoing plastic surgery?
2. What are the most popular cosmetic surgery procedures among teen patients, according to Coffey?
3. According to the author, what is the age requirement for breast augmentation?

Laura T. Coffey, "Can Plastic Surgery Be Good for Teens?," Today.com, March 30, 2010. Copyright © 2010 by Today.com. All rights reserved. Reproduced by permission.

Teens can be mean. Just ask Jen Selter, Jon Escalante and Hannah Olson.

For years, Selter endured taunts because of her nose size. Kids ridiculed her by saying she looked like a pelican and by calling her "butter face"—code for "She's hot, but her face!"

Escalante deliberately grew his hair out to hide ears that had branded him with the nickname "Dumbo." And Olson's self-confidence flagged as she tolerated "horrifying" name-calling after developing DDD-size breasts as a teen.

In a world where people of all ages increasingly turn to plastic surgery for reasons that are purely cosmetic—and, in some cases, narcissistic—Selter, Escalante and Olson said they opted to go under the knife as teenagers for different reasons. It wasn't something they did solely because of the relentless name-calling. It also had a whole lot to do with how they felt about themselves on a deeper level.

"My advice to teenagers is don't have a nose job just 'cause you're worried about what other people say or think," said Selter, who had rhinoplasty done last summer at age 15. "It all has to do with how you feel on the inside. And getting a nose job made me feel good inside and out."

Like "Braces for Crooked Teeth"?

To be sure, the very notion of doing any kind of plastic surgery on teenagers raises concerns for many parents and health professionals— and there are valid reasons for concern.

"Mom and Dad, please be sure your adolescent or your teen is aware that this is not a coping skill—that every time we feel uncomfortable about ourselves, then we go out and we get surgery," psychiatrist Charles Sophy told TODAY. "Because that's how we begin a huge line of problems."

Reputable cosmetic surgeons with teen patients typically recommend a series of at least four sessions with a therapist before moving forward with any procedures. The point of these sessions is to uncover underlying motives for wanting surgery, as well as to determine the emotional maturity of the patient.

Such precautionary steps are important because demand is on the rise. Although just two percent of all plastic surgeries are performed

Breast augmentation procedures performed in women 17 and under, by reason for surgery

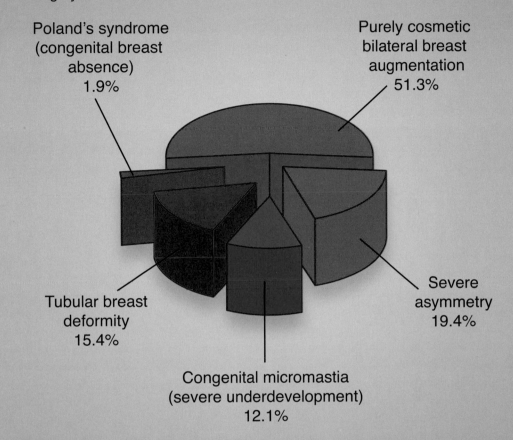

Poland's syndrome (congenital breast absence)
1.9%

Purely cosmetic bilateral breast augmentation
51.3%

Tubular breast deformity
15.4%

Severe asymmetry
19.4%

Congenital micromastia (severe underdevelopment)
12.1%

Notes: In 2013, there were 3,325 procedures performed on women 18 and under, about 1% of the total number of breast augmentations. The FDA recommends that cosmetic breast augmentation be restricted to women age 18 and above.

Taken from: Cosmetic Surgery National Data Bank Statistics, "2013 Age Distribution for Cosmetic Procedures," American Society for Aesthetic Plastic Surgery, 2013.

on teens, the number of teens getting plastic surgery has doubled since 2002, according to the American Society of Plastic Surgeons. Nose reshaping, ear reshaping, acne and acne-scar treatment, breast augmentation and breast reduction are popular procedures among teenage patients.

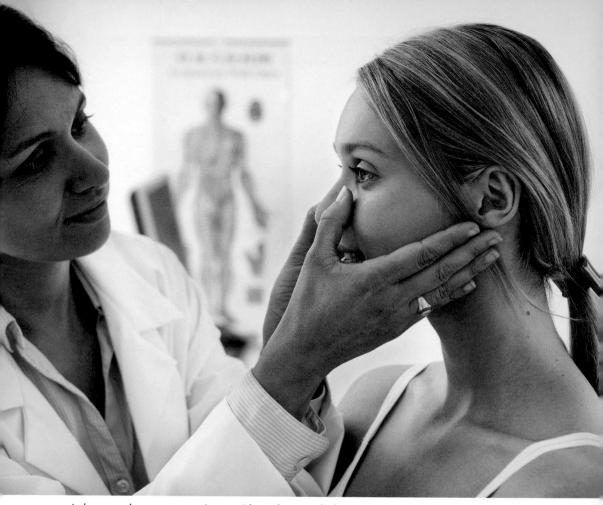

A doctor evaluates a patient's nose. Rhinoplasty might be an appropriate option for teens who cannot breathe through their nose properly.

Generally speaking, plastic surgeons report that many teens want plastic surgery because they long to fit in with their friends, while many adults pursue plastic surgery because they want to stand out.

But when a teen seeks out plastic surgery to correct a noticeable physical defect or to change a body part that's caused prolonged psychological distress, that can be a good thing, doctors say.

"It's no different than kids getting braces for crooked teeth," said Dr. Sam Rizk, Selter's plastic surgeon.

Dr. Nancy Snyderman, NBC's chief medical editor, agreed that plastic surgery can be altogether positive in the right circumstances. In the cases of Selter, Escalante and Olson—all of whom were featured in Friday's edition of *People* magazine and interviewed on TODAY on Tuesday—Snyderman thought they made responsible choices when they decided to have plastic surgery done at ages 15, 17 and 19.

"Remember we're not looking at 10- and 11-year-olds," Snyderman said. "We're looking at young adults who were part of the decision-making process, and that plays a big role. . . . You're looking at three very appropriate cases for wanting to change things."

How Young Is Too Young?

Before moving ahead with any kind of plastic surgery, parents and teens are encouraged to remember that surgeries are never risk-free. They should read up about any possible complications and be sure they can handle the risks involved. A real awareness of the risks can prompt parents and children to pursue non-surgical options for changing body image, such as diet and exercise.

Parents and children also should be aware that guidelines do exist for younger patients. Facial plastic surgery generally should not be done on anyone until facial growth is complete. For a female, that happens by about age 14; for a male, it's about age 15.

The U.S. Food and Drug Administration will not allow breast augmentation to be done on anyone younger than 18, and most surgeons will refuse to perform liposuction on anyone younger than 17 or 18.

(Generally speaking, it can be wise to choose a surgeon who has experience working with younger patients. Be sure to check the surgeon's complaint history.)

For their parts, Escalante, Olson and Selter all told TODAY that they have no regrets about their plastic surgeries. Escalante's decision to have his ears pinned back made him feel good about

> **FAST FACT**
>
> **Teens aged thirteen to nineteen accounted for 14 percent of all nose-reshaping procedures in the United States in 2012, according to the American Society of Plastic Surgeons.**

cutting his hair to pursue his dream of becoming a firefighter. Olson's breast-reduction surgery gave her relief from pain and made it possible to maintain an active, athletic lifestyle. And Selter's nose job made her more confident and carefree.

"Jen is so happy now," said Selter's mother, Jill Weinstein. "I would say to parents . . . it's the greatest gift you could give to your child. What greater gift is confidence and to help them feel happy in who they are?"

EVALUATING THE AUTHOR'S ARGUMENTS

In this viewpoint, Laura T. Coffey claims that cosmetic surgery can be beneficial for teens in some circumstances. Do you think teens having cosmetic surgery is an issue to be concerned about? Why or why not?

Cosmetic Surgery Is Not the Solution to Bullying

SidneyRose Reynen

"To seek help in the form of cosmetic surgery is just letting the bullies win."

In the following viewpoint, SidneyRose Reynen argues that cosmetic surgery is not the solution to bullying. The author highlights the nonprofit Little Baby Face, which offers free plastic surgery for bullied students. Encouraging teens to undergo plastic surgery to combat bullying puts the blame on the victims instead of the bullies, Reynen says. She maintains that cosmetic surgery will not improve the mental state of emotionally scarred children. Instead of focusing on appearance, the author contends that adults should encourage teens to devote themselves to their schoolwork, communities, and self-care. At the time of this viewpoint, Reynen was a film and art history student at Louisiana State University in Baton Rouge, Louisiana.

AS YOU READ, CONSIDER THE FOLLOWING QUESTIONS:

1. According to the author, whom does Little Baby Face provide free plastic surgery for?

SidneyRose Reynen, "Opinion: Cosmetic Surgery Is Not the Solution to Bullying," *Daily Reveille*, February 26, 2014. Copyright © 2014 by Louisiana State University Press. All rights reserved. Reproduced by permission.

2. Little Baby Face has provided surgery for how many children since 2002, according to the author?
3. What happens when bullied children are encouraged to seek cosmetic surgery, as stated by Reynen?

Were you ever bullied as a kid? Maybe you should have gotten a nose job.

Even though that sounds like an outrageous solution, the New York–based nonprofit organization Little Baby Face provides free plastic surgery for bullied middle and high school students.

The Little Baby Face Foundation is teaching kids that if they want to stop being bullied, then *they* should change—not the bullies.

Little Baby Face operated on a 14-year-old girl in 2012. They paid for surgery that she requested—an operation that would pin her ears back because kids at Ilse's school had been referring to her as "Dumbo."

More recently, the nonprofit provided a 15-year-old with a rhinoplasty [nose job] and a chin job. She was known by her classmates as "the girl with the big nose." The teasing had become so intense and pervasive that she did not attend school for three years, opting to be home-schooled instead.

On its website, Little Baby Face says it was "born out of the desire to serve and assist children with birth deformities and their families that are without resources by providing them with the life-changing restorative treatments and surgeries free of cost." It also claims to have "helped" more than 500 children with facial deformities since it was founded in 2002.

While I certainly feel immense sympathy for these emotionally scarred children, I don't believe this is the way to help them.

Getting Cosmetic Surgery Lets the Bullies Win

There has to be nothing worse than submitting a request to this organization and then being approved for surgery. It's almost as if the Little Baby Face Foundation is agreeing with the bullies' thinking.

This fascination with cosmetic surgery has invaded cities other than Los Angeles and Hollywood. Not only can these young children receive "life changing" operations, so can anyone in Baton Rouge. With a quick Google search, one can find that there are more than 30 different cosmetic surgery and dentistry offices within a 10-mile radius of the University.

Feeling left out on such a large campus? Buy yourself a new face!

Bullying is not a new phenomenon, nor is it one that affects only a small population of people.

FAST FACT

The American Society of Plastic Surgeons reports that cosmetic procedures for thirteen- to nineteen-year-olds represented 2 percent of all procedures performed in 2013.

During my time in elementary, middle and high school, classmates made fun of everything from my bad acne to the size of my breasts to the fact that I wore glasses. This is not an experience unknown to most.

The occurrence of bullying and the overall mean-natured spirit of children and adolescents is not something to blow off as being "just what kids do." Teasing fellow students about their physical appearance perpetuates and demonstrates our unnatural obsession with beauty.

Encouraging bullied children and teenagers to seek help in the form of cosmetic surgery is just letting the bullies win. They don't learn anything from their mistakes or suffering, but hey—there's a brand new nose involved, so why complain?

Self Care Is More Important than Cosmetic Surgery

Bullies are the ones who need to change their ways. Kids who think it's funny to prey on classmates to make them feel alienated and ugly are what needs to be corrected, not some young girl's protruding ears.

Although the Little Baby Face Foundation helps underprivileged children with facial deformities—real ones, not just noses deemed unattractively large—that hinder them from performing daily tasks or communicating, it's a shame this has become an option for America's youngest generation.

Apparently, if the public has a problem with you, then you should do everything in your power to change yourself to conform to their standards.

Cosmetic Procedures for Teens

Surgical and nonsurgical procedures performed on persons ages 13 to 19 in 2011 and percentage change from 2010.

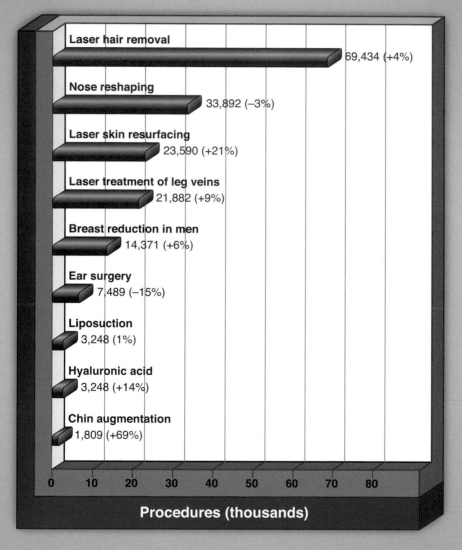

Taken from: "US Plastic Surgery Statistics: Chins, Buttocks, and Breasts Up, Ears Down," *The Guardian* (UK), 2011.

The attitude should not be "above all—be attractive." Kids and adolescents should strive for better grades, more involvement in their communities and self-care rather than being aesthetically pleasing to everyone they meet.

As Beyoncé says in her song "Pretty Hurts," "It's the soul that needs the surgery."

EVALUATING THE AUTHOR'S ARGUMENTS

In this viewpoint, SidneyRose Reynen argues that a nonprofit that offers free plastic surgery to bullied students is not helping them. Do you believe the nonprofit's efforts are beneficial or harmful to students? Why?

Viewpoint 3

The Golden Years, Polished with Surgery

Abby Ellin

"People are living longer . . . and they want their physiques to align with their psyches."

In the following viewpoint, Abby Ellin explores the rising number of seniors who are undergoing cosmetic surgery procedures. She attributes this trend to the number of seniors who are living longer and thus want to enhance their appearance, those who are seeking potential mates, and those who are still working or are looking for employment and want to appear more youthful. Few studies have focused on elderly patients and plastic surgery, the author contends; however, she highlights research showing that the risks of surgery for those over sixty-five are not greater than for the younger population. Ellin writes the Vows column for the *New York Times*, and previously wrote the Preludes column about young people and money. She is also the author of *Teenage Waistland*, which addresses teen obesity.

AS YOU READ, CONSIDER THE FOLLOWING QUESTIONS:

1. In 2010 there were how many surgical procedures among patients older than sixty-five, according to the author?

Abby Ellin, "The Golden Years, Polished with Surgery." From the *New York Times*, August 8, 2011. Copyright © 2011 The New York Times. All rights reserved. Used by permission and protected by the Copyright Laws of the United States. The printing, copying, redistribution, or retransmission of this Content without express written permission is prohibited.

2. Why do experts predict that the number of seniors undergoing plastic surgery will continue to rise?
3. According to a report by *Plastic and Reconstructive Surgery*, how do the risks of cosmetic surgery for those over sixty-five compare to those of the younger population?

At age 83, Marie Kolstad has a rich life. She works full time as a property manager and keeps an active social calendar, busying herself with 12 grandchildren and 13 great-grandchildren.

But one thing needed improvement, she decided: her figure. At her age, she said, "your breasts go in one direction and your brain goes in another." So on July 22, Ms. Kolstad, a widow who lives in Orange County, Calif., underwent a three-hour breast lift with implants, which costs about $8,000.

A woman discusses breast implant options with a plastic surgeon. A growing segment of senior citizens are opting for cosmetic surgery.

"Physically, I'm in good health, and I just feel like, why not take advantage of it?" said Ms. Kolstad. "My mother lived a long time, and I'm just taking it for granted that that will happen to me. And I want my children to be proud of what I look like.

The Increase in Cosmetic Surgeries Among Older Patients

Ms. Kolstad is one of many septuagenarians, octogenarians and even nonagenarians who are burnishing their golden years with help from the plastic surgeon. According to the American Society for Aesthetic Plastic Surgery, in 2010 there were 84,685 surgical procedures among patients age 65 and older. They included 26,635 face-lifts; 24,783 cosmetic eyelid operations; 6,469 liposuctions; 5,874 breast reductions;

Cosmetic Procedures for Patients Sixty-Five and Older

Procedure Type	Number of Procedures	Percent of Procedural Total
Surgical procedures (breast, face, neck, buttocks, arms, legs, tummy, etc.)	145,835	7.7%
Injectables (Botox, Radiesse, Sculptra, Artefil, etc.)	593,536	10.1%
Skin rejuvenation (chemical peels, dermabrasion, laser skin resurfacing, etc.)	285,950	13.3%
Other non-surgical procedures (cellulite treatment, hair removal, nonsurgical fat reduction, tattoo removal, leg veins, etc.)	76,920	5.2%

Taken from: Cosmetic Surgery National Data Bank Statistics, "2013 Age Distribution for Cosmetic Procedures," American Society for Aesthetic Plastic Surgery, 2013.

3,875 forehead lifts; 3,339 breast lifts and 2,414 breast augmentations.

Except for a brief turndown during the recession, those numbers have been rising for years now, and experts say the trend seems likely to accelerate as baby boomers begin to pass age 65. But the increase also has raised concerns about safety and the propriety of performing invasive elective surgery on older patients, who may suffer unintended physical and psychological consequences.

There are as many reasons for getting plastic surgery as there are older patients, experts say. Some people are living longer and remaining healthier, and they want their physiques to align with their psyches. Some are preening for potential mates and want their feathers to look their freshest. Some are still working or looking for jobs and want to be seen as more youthful contenders.

And some are simply sick of slackened jowls, jiggly underarms and saggy eyelids. Gilbert Meyer, a retired film producer in Boynton Beach, Fla., who gave his age only as "over 75," saw Dr. Jacob Steiger, a facial plastic surgeon in Boca Raton, Fla., for an eye and neck lift last year. He spent $8,000.

"I was looking at myself in the mirror and didn't like what I was starting to see and did something about it," Mr. Meyer said. "Why not look as good as you can when you can?"

Mary Graham, a 77-year-old restaurant owner in Thomasville, Ga., got a face-lift and breast implants earlier this year. "The only time I go to the doctor is for plastic surgery," she said.

Ms. Graham plans to open another restaurant in Tallahassee, Fla., in the fall. "I work seven days a week," she said. "I wanted to look as young as I feel."

Her plastic surgeon, Dr. Daniel Man of Boca Raton, Fla., who said he is seeing increasing numbers of patients over age 70, said, "These people are healthy and want to be an active part of society."

Examining the Risks of Surgery

Any operation poses risks, but surprisingly few studies have focused on older patients and cosmetic enhancements. One report, published in the journal *Plastic and Reconstructive Surgery* in June, found that the hazards in people over age 65 are no greater than in the younger population.

Researchers from the Cleveland Clinic reviewed the medical records of 216 face-lift patients over the course of three years. The researchers found no significant difference in the instances of minor or major complications between one group of patients whose average age was 70 and another group whose average age was 57.6.

"We're saying it's not chronologic age that's so important, but it really is physiologic," said Dr. James E. Zins, the senior author of the study and chairman of the department of plastic surgery at the Cleveland Clinic.

All patients in his study were screened for such health problems as lung and heart disease, diabetes and high blood pressure, as well as use of medications, like anticoagulants, that could have complicated the operations. But not all older patients may be so thoroughly screened, so his findings don't necessarily mean the risks are minimal in an older population.

FAST FACT

In 2013, the sixty-five-and-over age group had 9.7 percent of all cosmetic procedures, according to the American Society for Aesthetic Plastic Surgery.

"Is there a theoretical age upon which complications do become more likely?" he mused. "Does that mean that patients 70 and 75 years and over can safely undergo a face-lift with the same complication rate as young patients? We didn't have enough numbers to answer that question."

While face-lifts can be performed under "conscious sedation," other reconstructive procedures typically require general anesthesia, which may be risky for an elderly patient. Older patients may take longer to heal, and the results of plastic surgery may not last as long as in younger patients, said Dr. Michael Niccole, a plastic surgeon in Newport Beach, Calif.

Some critics question whether the benefits are worth the risks, which may be underestimated.

"You know there are biases because of the underreporting of negative findings," said James Hughes, executive director of the Institute for Ethics and Emerging Technologies, a nonprofit research group in Hartford. "The doctors have more or less financial incentives to do these procedures, and that often leads them to understate alternative kinds of treatments or medical advice."

Harriet A. Washington, author of two books about medical ethics issues, asks how older patients can give informed consent to plastic surgery when so little is known of its risks to them, especially to those with chronic conditions like diabetes, osteoporosis and heart disease.

"It's one of those things that has crept up on us, and I think, as usual, we've embraced the technology before we've really embraced the ethical questions and dimensions," she said.

And while most research indicates that people benefit psychologically from cosmetic procedures, reporting improvements in their appearance and in body image, a minority experience some kind of emotional "turbulence," said David Sarwer, an associate professor of psychology at the University of Pennsylvania School of Medicine.

"There are truly psychological repercussions to these procedures, which often aren't covered in the informed consent process," he said.

Tackling the Stereotypes of Aging

And yet: Assuming a patient is healthy, meets all of the presurgical criteria and understands that there are risks, why is it people often are squeamish about seniors going under the knife?

Nancy Etcoff, an assistant clinical professor at Harvard Medical School who studies biology and social beliefs about beauty, believes the double takes arise from our culture's mixed feelings about old people actively on the prowl. "Part of our stereotype of old people is that they are social, warm and likeable, but powerless and sexless," she said. "Here we are in the age of Viagra, which is very well accepted, but suddenly the idea of older people, mostly women, wanting to be sexually attractive at that age makes us uncomfortable.

"If an older woman wants to regain eyelids or wants a breast that she doesn't have to tuck into a waistband, then why not?"

Ms. Kolstad asked herself much the same question. "In my day, no one ever thought about breast enhancement or anything," she said. "But nowadays women go out and they would never get a second look if they show their age. I find that you have to keep up your appearance physically, even if you just want a companion or someone to ask you to dinner.

"That's not going to happen if you don't have a figure that these geezers are looking for."

EVALUATING THE AUTHOR'S ARGUMENTS

In this viewpoint, Abby Ellin claims that few studies have focused on elderly patients and cosmetic surgery, but research shows there are no increased risks caused by age. What reasons can you think of for arguing that cosmetic surgery could pose *more* health risks for elderly patients?

My Plastic Surgery Regrets

Michele Willens

"Cosmetic changes may seem superficial but they . . . have far-reaching emotional consequences."

In the following viewpoint, Michele Willens argues that cosmetic surgery is not the solution to battling the outward effects of growing older. She relates her experience with cosmetic surgery as well as that of one of her friends. While her friend's procedure resulted in harmful physical effects, the author explains that her own surgery took a psychological toll. Ultimately the author was disappointed with the outcome of her surgery and would not choose to go through the experience again. Willens writes for the *Huffington Post*, Daily Beast, and *The Atlantic*. She is also the editor of the book *Face It: What Women Really Feel as Their Looks Change*.

AS YOU READ, CONSIDER THE FOLLOWING QUESTIONS:

1. In 2012, how many patients underwent a cosmetic procedure in the United States, according to the author?
2. What is the demographic of most cosmetic surgery patients, as stated by Willens?
3. According to the author, how many baby boomers would have cosmetic surgery if they could afford it?

Michele Willens, "My Plastic Surgery Regrets." From the Daily Beast, May 23, 2013. Copyright © 2013 The Daily Beast Company LLC. All rights reserved. Used by permission and protected by the Copyright Laws of the United States. The printing, copying, redistribution, or retransmission of this Content without express written permission is prohibited.

On this very website, Samantha Marshall touted the success she has had with numerous cosmetic surgeries. I am thrilled for her, but lately, I have run into—and experienced—more and more disenchantment on the subject. I had some work done on my neck and chin area about a year and a half ago. Barbara, my downstairs neighbor, had a similar procedure in January. We both had six very good, satisfied weeks. Since then, she has been suffering one medical mishap after another. My repercussions have been mostly of the mental variety.

There are 79 million baby boomers now hitting the age when our mothers were blushingly asked, "Did she or didn't she?" and were happily settling into retirement and grandparenthood. As for us, we are desperately seeking ways to stay vital as we face what we are told will

Uneven sagging of the skin after a face-lift, as can be seen on the right of this image of a patient's face, is one of the possible side effects or complications of the surgery.

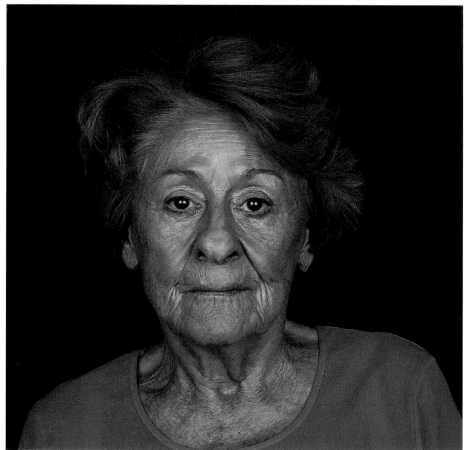

be an unprecedented 30 more years or so of a "second adulthood." As OB-GYN Dr. Rebecca Brightman says, "Keep in mind that 40 percent of women's lives now take place beyond menopause." Damned if I am doing three decades with gray hair and jowls.

Barbara and I are not alone in using our former anti-war fervor to take on aging. Over 11 million Americans had some form of cosmetic procedure; 17 percent of those were actual surgeries. (Those also accounted for 61 percent of the expenditures.) It is no surprise that 90 percent of the patients are female, with the majority being married, college educated, employed mothers. While a growing number of younger women and even teens are having plastic surgery, most patients are between the ages of 35 and 65.

There are no concrete statistics, however, on the number of those satisfied (like Samantha Marshall) or those who subsequently hopped onto a slippery slope (like Samantha Marshall). You know—you get a new dining table and suddenly those chairs look awfully old. Not to mention those, like my neighbor Barbara, who have real medical complications of some sort from surgery. "What they don't publicize is what I hear," says Dr. Brightman, "which is revisions, revisions, revisions."

Aside from Barbara, one friend told me she had to have her eye job repeated six months later; two had to have their faces done again; and yet another's procedure left her with a drooping eye that needed repair. Leslie, a performer friend, says she was at first "thrilled to get my chin off my neck, and relieved to have eyelids. Yet it wasn't long after, that I noticed one side starting to sag. The doctor wasn't at all happy with the results and wound up doing the whole thing again! The hardest part was the swelling and my husband says I looked cross-eyed for a long time. I am glad I did it, but wish I'd known it would take two years for the swelling to really go down."

Then you throw in the guilt, the embarrassment, and the disappointment that life pretty much goes on as it was. "When contemplating physical changes to your face and body, it goes without saying that there are risks that must be considered, and not just physical ones," says New York psychologist Dr. Vivian Diller. "Cosmetic changes may seem superficial but they are permanent and have far-reaching emotional consequences." Dr. Diller (with whom I worked on a book on helping women navigate the aging process) talks many patients

"At the time, Botox seemed like a good idea, but now I can't smile," cartoon by Marty Bucella, www
.CartoonStock.com. Copyright © Marty Bucella. Reproduction rights obtainable from www.CartoonStock
.com.

through their conflicting feelings over the decision, asking what they
expect in return, and for whom they are really doing it.

The public's reaction to the subject is often as unpredictable as the
procedures. When Jane Fonda proudly touted her "good work" to
Oprah, the audience roundly applauded. Remember when a country-
full of women supported Betty Ford's very public First Facelift? Yet,
how would they feel if Hillary had one before 2016? We all whisper
about Nicole and Meg and Stockard and Goldie, yet I have the feeling
we'd feel somewhat betrayed if Meryl or Helen came forward with
news of a nip-and-tuck. Jamie Lee—a heroine for letting the cellu-
lite et al. show—admitted to some work awhile back and then flatly
stated, "none of it works."

Whether in the public eye, or privately seeing ourselves through
our own distorted ones (more than six million viewers watched a

YouTube video of a Dove advertising campaign in which women harshly describe their appearance to a forensic sketch artist) we tend to be our toughest critics. "The ability to reduce judgment is an essential element in therapy," says Brooklyn psychologist Gretta Keene. "Letting go is a powerful tool when people are locked into images of how their faces or bodies should be."

Needless to say, the industry's associations such as the American Society of Plastic Surgeons, have no records of surgeries gone wrong. Though when Kanye West lost his 58-year-old mother following cosmetic surgery, we did hear about it loud and clear. Kanye has access to a megaphone, of course, unlike one Minerva Rodriguez, who died shortly after a "buttock augmentation" in February in Washington Heights in NYC. (Diagnosed later as poisoned by acute idocaine intoxication.) I have no doubt that far more go right than wrong. "Those are really the exceptions, most are happy patients," says NY dermatologist Dr. Doris Day. "I am sending patients out to plastic surgeons every day, but I do warn them to be realistic about their expectations. And I am strongly against before and after photos of others, because everyone looks different."

Barbara was only interested in the wrinkles on her neck and if you just focus on that now—and her rejuvenated cheeks from injections during the procedure—she looks far younger than her 69 years. Unfortunately, you have to get past the half dozen cysts on her face and the parotid gland in her neck that erupted about a month after her surgery. She has spent $1,200 on visits to the dermatologist (to drain the abscesses), and has paid visits to an ENT physician and most recently, an infectious disease specialist who, at least, has come up with some kind of diagnosis: a mycobacterium infection that all agree was somehow picked up during the surgery or in the operating room.

Barbara is a sunny personality by nature, though she admits she has broken down crying recently. She takes some mild pleasure in the fact that all the doctors are conferring with one another "and I am being treated as a very special case." For now—and likely for at least another six months—she is on heavily prescribed medications and relies on Band-Aids and plenty of makeup.

My wounds, such as they are, cannot be covered with anything.

This was not a decision made without serious self-interrogation. Can I be a feminist and narcissist at the same time? Have I turned into *that* woman? Who will I tell? This may be politically palatable rationalization, but I do believe that I did it for the right reasons. Part of my lower face was sagging—a congenital condition, I was told—(when in doubt, blame Mom and Dad) and frankly, did not reflect how I felt and how the rest of my body looked. In the end, I felt clear and strong, did not mind the procedure—in fact, enjoyed the alone recovery time—and hardly bruised at all.

Within weeks, I was being told how great I looked and I rocked at my 45th high school reunion. (Which I promise did not spur my decision.) I was not known in adolescence for my looks—which were always fine, but not Prom Princess fine. I am well aware that the process is very often toughest on those who *did* rely on their God-given beauty. The rest of us had to compensate in other ways and perhaps that makes these years somewhat more manageable.

The doctor told me what I could expect—sort of: when the stitches would come out, when I could exercise again, how long there would be tightness in the neck, etc. While not having the side effects that Barbara is experiencing, I did soon after get some darkened spots which the good doctor claims are sun damage, not related to the surgery. (Nevertheless he continues to try to laser them away.) What he didn't tell me was that I would be tingly and numb for a long time and that I would be wracked with emotional ups and downs. Only on one of many subsequent visits, as I confessed I was having a difficult time on many levels, did he use the word "insidious" for what I had undergone.

> ## FAST FACT
>
> According to the *Huffington Post*, the average cost of a cosmetic surgical procedure in the United States is $3,694.

I ask Barbara why she isn't pressing her surgeon to take more responsibility. Then again, I find myself being seduced and intimidated by mine, who keeps nodding, reassuring and lasering. Do we not *lean in* at the doctor's office either?

Am I angry? Consider that I wrote a one-act play called *Waiting for Dr. Hoffman*, wherein three ambivalent women in a cosmetic surgeon's office are shocked when a former patient barges in, armed and demanding a do-over. When it was performed in Los Angeles and

New York last year, people assumed the sarcastic writer character "just here for a consultation" was based on me. No one suspected I might be the girl with the gun.

The emotions are far more complicated. I did this not to look younger so much as to feel better, but ended up liking that I also looked younger. I am guilt-ridden that this stuff matters when others have real health, family, and economic issues. (Though a Harris Poll revealed that two thirds of the boomer-aged participants would do some cosmetic work if they could afford it.) I am frustrated in that I am not sure where the money went. And I am amazed when I recall that as a 21-year-old journalist, I wrote a hotly debated article in which I worried that my big breasts were making me suspicious of men's interest. Here, 40 years later, I am still writing about my body.

Finally, it is depressing that while women have made so many strides in so many aspects of our lives, we can't get a grip on this one. There are some glimmers of hope for, if not a reverse of the cosmetic trend, at least a tempering of it. Both Dr. Diller and Dr. Brightman have been asked to consult for top cosmetic companies seeking to understand the needs of women midlife and beyond. "I am sensing somewhat less of a rush to run out and get work done," says Dr. Brightman. "And when they do, it may be the less invasive kind or an attempt for a more natural look."

The million-dollar question, of course, is, "are you glad you did it"? Barbara says flatly, "I would not do it again, knowing I had to go through this." For me, the brutal truth is it has been a lousy year and a half. But those six weeks were sure fun.

EVALUATING THE AUTHOR'S ARGUMENTS

In this viewpoint, Michele Willens claims that cosmetic surgery can have damaging physical and emotional effects for older patients. Whose experiences do you find more convincing, those in this viewpoint or those in Abby Ellin's viewpoint? Explain.

Botox as a Career-Builder for Boomer Men

Elizabeth O'Brien

"Workplace concerns have been particularly influential in driving male patients to . . . cosmetic procedures."

In the following viewpoint, Elizabeth O'Brien explores the rising trend of men undergoing cosmetic surgery. The majority of the men are seeking facial fillers that minimize the appearance of wrinkles, the author contends. She attributes this phenomenon to the competitive job market. The author cites research about age discrimination in the workplace and states that it takes job seekers over the age of fifty-five much longer to find work if they lose their jobs. Men who are getting cosmetic surgery want to appear more youthful, the author says, as well as achieve job security. O'Brien is a retirement reporter for MarketWatch, a website of the *Wall Street Journal*.

AS YOU READ, CONSIDER THE FOLLOWING QUESTIONS:

1. According to the author, what was the percentage rise in cosmetic procedures for men from 2000 to 2012?
2. O'Brien states that the average duration of unemployment for job seekers older than fifty-five is how long?
3. What percentage of cosmetic procedure patients are men, according to the author?

Elizabeth O'Brien, "Botox as a Career-Builder for Boomer Men," MarketWatch, October 16, 2013. Copyright © 2013 by MarketWatch, Inc. All rights reserved. Reproduced by permission.

D r. David McDaniel, a dermatologist in Virginia Beach, Va., recalled an awkward scene a while back when a husband bumped into his wife at McDaniel's office. Both were there for Botox, but the husband hadn't told his wife he was getting treated. The man quickly threw his arm around McDaniel, pretending the doctor was an old buddy who he had stopped by to visit. "Men are stealthy," McDaniel said.

However stealthily, men are having a little work done in increasing numbers these days, plastic surgeons and dermatologists report. Total cosmetic procedures for men rose 22% from 2000 through 2012, according to the American Society of Plastic Surgeons. From 2011 to 2012, men's use of minimally invasive cosmetic procedures such as botulinum toxin (sold under the brand name Botox) rose 6%, according to the society.

Top Five Minimally Invasive Procedures for Men

Procedure	Number
Botulinum toxin (Botox)	363,018
Laser hair removal	185,577
Microdermabrasion	165,624
Chemical peel	87,851
Soft tissue fillers	86,794

Number of procedures (thousands)

Total procedures: 989,644

Taken from: "US Plastic Surgery Statistics: Chins, Buttocks, and Breasts Up, Ears Down," *The Guardian* (UK), 2011.

Underlying this trend at the doctor's office, practitioners say, is a harsh reality in the workplace. While the unemployment rate for those 55 and over is lower than for other ages, it takes boomers much longer to find work if they lose their jobs. The duration of unemployment for job seekers 55 and over is 50.4 weeks, compared with 34.2 weeks for those under 55, according to an analysis of BLS data by Sara Rix of the AARP Public Policy Institute.

And there's evidence that, despite laws prohibiting age discrimination, looking old (or at least looking older) can hamper efforts to reboot a career. "Appearance matters in a job search," said John Challenger, CEO of Challenger, Gray & Christmas, a Chicago-based global outplacement firm.

With all this mind, men are visiting plastic surgeons and dermatologists for Botox and facial fillers that minimize the appearance of wrinkles. Women visit too, of course, and face similar pressures at work. But some doctors say workplace concerns have been particularly influential in driving male patients to get past the stigma some men attach to cosmetic procedures. (While their ranks are growing, men still make up just 9% of overall cosmetic procedure patients, according to the American Society of Plastic Surgeons.)

FAST FACT

The American Academy of Facial Plastic and Reconstructive Surgery estimates that 21 percent of male patients choose plastic surgery as a result of their partner's having done it.

McDaniel said a couple of years ago he had many 50-something, male middle managers coming to him because they were worried about keeping their jobs. While such visits have tapered off somewhat with the improving economy, McDaniel still sees plenty of guys these days. He does laser skin resurfacing on the faces of men who have done too many sunblock-less rounds on the golf course, and he sees men in their early 30s for "pre-juvenation," or treatments such as microdermabrasion designed to delay the onset of wrinkles.

The good news, Challenger said, is that there are plenty of ways to come across as youthful in a job interview. A 55-year-old candidate who projects an energetic vibe can go a long way toward eas-

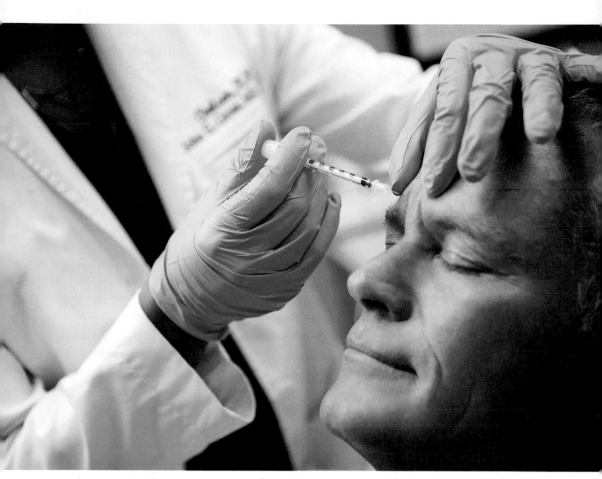

A man receives Botox treatment at a clinic. More men over age fifty are seeking minimally invasive cosmetic procedures, such as Botox injections or skin rejuvenation.

ing prospective employers' concerns about his age, Challenger said. Challenger said he wouldn't advise a client one way or another about using cosmetic procedures to attain that vibe. But he said he counsels older job seekers against omitting signs of their age, such as their college graduation year, from their resume: "If it's not there, they know there's a reason or it."

Paying Out of Pocket

Cosmetic treatments generally aren't covered by health insurance plans, and they don't come cheap. Botox is typically sold either by the unit or per "treatment area"—a dosage for crows' feet, for example. One unit costs around $15, Dr. J. Shah, a doctor of antiaging medicine and the chief medical director of Amari Medical in Scarsdale, N.Y. Areas might cost $200 or more to treat (treating laugh lines around the eyes alone would cost less than laugh lines plus forehead and frown lines, for example). Fillers are sold by the syringe and typically run $500 to $600 per vial, with a usual minimum of 2 shots per treatment, Shah said.

Here's the catch: These are hardly one-time expenses. Like gray roots, wrinkles resurface. Botox typically lasts about three months, while fillers can last about a year, Shah said.

If such treatments help a man hang on to a well-paying job with benefits, he might consider them a very worthy investment, although ultimately, of course, that's a matter of individual choice.

Note to guys who decide to proceed: Don't shop for cosmetic procedures like you shop for cars. It isn't a matter of getting the best price for a menu of features, experts say. Fillers and Botox are not commodities that perform the same no matter who injects them, and even "minimally invasive" procedures can go wrong in unskilled hands (think a frozen look from bad Botox, or "duck lips" from too much filler, to name just a couple of examples).

Dermatologists and plastic surgeons have plenty of competition these days when it comes to administering cosmetic treatments, from everyone from dentists to medical spa technicians who aren't doctors or even nurses. Unsurprisingly, experts say the doctors who get the best results tend to be those who specialize in cosmetic procedures and do them all day long.

Next Up: A Face-Lift?

Some doctors also advise that patients go to a practitioner who offers a full range of cosmetic treatments, from minimally invasive to more involved procedures, such as face-lifts. Dr. Eric Swanson, a member of the American Society for Aesthetic Plastic Surgery and a practicing plastic surgeon in Kansas City, Kan., sees men in their mid-60s who want to get rid of their "turkey wattle." In these cases, he said, injections usually aren't the answer and a face-lift is needed instead.

Of course, face-lifts are pricier, running anywhere between $8,000 in low-cost parts of the country to the $20,000 charged by some New

York City or Beverly Hills doctors. Such procedures last longer, but require more down time, which may be tough to fit in to an executive's schedule. For his part, Swanson thinks patients are fine with this: "They want results."

EVALUATING THE AUTHOR'S ARGUMENTS

In this viewpoint, Elizabeth O'Brien claims that a rising number of men are seeking cosmetic procedures for job security. Why might someone argue that undergoing cosmetic surgery will not help men in the workplace?

Facts About Cosmetic Surgery

Editor's note: These facts can be used in reports to add credibility when making important points or claims.

Medical Tourism

According to Patients Beyond Borders:

- The top destinations worldwide for medical tourism are Brazil, Costa Rica, India, Malaysia, Mexico, Singapore, South Korea, Taiwan, Thailand, Turkey, and the United States.
- Based on an estimated 11 million patients worldwide crossing a border for medical care each year, the estimated medical tourism market size is $38.5–$55 billion.

According to Reuters:

- In a survey of people from twenty-four countries, those from Japan, South Korea, Spain, and Sweden were least likely to be medical tourists.
- Those most likely to consider medical tourism in the same survey were Indians, Indonesians, Russians, Mexicans, and Poles.

According to the Centers for Disease Control and Prevention:

- Estimates suggest that up to 750,000 US residents travel abroad for medical treatment each year.

According to the Organisation for Economic Co-operation and Development:

- In one study, 37 percent of British cosmetic surgeons surveyed reported having treated patients with complications resulting from overseas cosmetic surgery.

Cosmetic Surgery Around the World

According to the International Society for Aesthetic Plastic Surgeons:

- The United States and Brazil performed an estimated 21.1 percent and 9.8 percent, respectively, of all surgical and nonsurgical cosmetic procedures worldwide in 2011, making them the top two nations in terms of total procedures performed.
- The continent where the most procedures were carried out was Asia, where 29.5 percent of all surgical and nonsurgical procedures took place in 2011. North America was a close 28.5 percent.
- In total numbers of surgical and nonsurgical cosmetic procedures performed, Africa has one of the lowest counts, with only 1.6 percent of all procedures in 2011.
- Oceania has the lowest count, with 0.9 percent of all procedures worldwide.
- Of the European countries, Italy performed the most cosmetic procedures in 2011, with 4.8 percent of the worldwide share. Second and third in Europe were France (3.1 percent) and Germany (2.8 percent).
- The most commonly performed cosmetic surgical procedure in the world in 2011 was liposuction—the surgical removal of fat. Liposuction procedures represented 19.9 percent of all procedures worldwide, followed by breast augmentation (18.9 percent) and surgery on the eyelid, called blepharoplasty (11 percent).
- China and Japan performed the most nose jobs in 2011, cornering 10.8 percent and 9.7 percent of the worldwide share, respectively.

According to Business Insider:

- The US city with the most board-certified plastic surgeons per capita in 2014 was Salt Lake City, Utah, with 4.89 surgeons per hundred thousand people. Miami, Florida, ranked second, with 4.62, and San Francisco, California, was third, with 3.88.

Demographics of Cosmetic Surgery

According to the American Society for Aesthetic Plastic Surgery:

- Women are slightly more accepting of cosmetic surgery than men in the United States, with 53 percent of women approving vs. 49 percent of men.
- Unmarried Americans are slightly more likely to consider cosmetic surgery than their married counterparts; 33 percent of unmarried Americans would consider it vs. 27 percent for those who are married.
- Twenty percent of Americans in 2011 had a more favorable attitude toward cosmetic surgery than they had held five years earlier, while 71 percent had no change in attitude.
- Thirty-seven percent of eighteen- to twenty-four-year-olds reported considering cosmetic surgery for themselves, making them the age group most likely to consider it.
- Of the sixty-five and older set, 77 percent would not be embarrassed about getting cosmetic surgery.
- At 56 percent approving, the highest income earners (making more than $75,000 a year) show the greatest approval rate for cosmetic surgery of all income groups. The lowest earners (making less than $25,000 annually) approve 52 percent of the time, and the middle-income groups approve 48 percent of the time among those earning $25,000–$50,000 and 45 percent of the time among those earning $50,000–$75,000.

Spending on Cosmetic Surgery

According to the American Society for Aesthetic Plastic Surgery:

- In 2013 surgical procedures made up 16.5 percent of all cosmetic procedures performed and 58 percent of total spending on cosmetic procedures in the United States. Nonsurgical procedures made up 83.5 percent of all cosmetic procedures and accounted for 42 percent of total spending.
- Americans' total spending on cosmetic procedures in 2013 topped $12 billion, over $7 billion of which went to surgical procedures and over $5 billion to nonsurgical procedures.

According to the American Society of Plastic Surgeons:

- The two most expensive cosmetic surgical procedures in the United States in 2013 were the lower body lift, averaging $8,144 per operation, and the facelift, averaging $6,556.
- The cheapest operations in 2013, on average, were dermabrasion, costing $1,151 and lip reduction, at $1,443.
- As for nonsurgical cosmetic procedures, the most expensive options in 2013 were laser skin resurfacing, which could cost up to $2,157 on average, and soft tissue fillers, which can cost as much as $1,682.
- At the lowest end of the nonsurgical cosmetic procedures are microdermabrasion, which averages $148, and cellulite treatment, at $245.

Organizations to Contact

The editors have compiled the following list of organizations concerned with the issues debated in this book. The descriptions are derived from materials provided by the organizations. All have publications or information available for interested readers. The list was compiled on the date of publication of the present volume; the information provided here may change. Be aware that many organizations take several weeks or longer to respond to inquiries, so allow as much time as possible for the receipt of requested materials.

American Academy of Cosmetic Surgery (AACS)
303 W. Madison Street, Suite 2650
Chicago, IL 60606
(312) 981-6760 • fax: (312) 265-2908
e-mail: info@cosmeticsurgery.org
website: www.cosmeticsurgery.org

The American Academy of Cosmetic Surgery is a nonprofit corporation that focuses on furthering the education of professionals in the field of cosmetic surgery. The organization also fosters partnerships with corporations and academic institutions. The vision of the AACS is "to become recognized as the leader in cosmetic surgery who possesses the values, competencies and resources necessary to drive patient safety throughout the industry." The organization was founded in 1985 when three existing cosmetic surgery societies united with the goal of encouraging plastic surgeons to teach and learn from each other. Today the AACS boasts approximately two thousand members and publishes two journals: *Surge* and the *American Journal of Cosmetic Surgery*.

American Academy of Facial Plastic and Reconstructive Surgery (AAFPRS)
310 S. Henry Street
Alexandria, VA 22314
(703) 299-9291 • fax: (703) 299-8898
e-mail: info@aafprs.org

website: www.aafprs.org

With a membership of twenty-seven hundred board-certified facial plastic and reconstructive surgeons, the American Academy of Facial Plastic and Reconstructive Surgery is the largest facial plastic surgery association in the world. Members specialize in surgery of the face, head, and neck and are certified by any of several specialty boards recognized by the American Board of Medical Specialties. The organization was formed in 1964 with a focus on creating training opportunities and promoting recognition of facial plastic surgeons' expertise. The organization's mission statement also emphasizes the promotion of high ethical standards among its members and a focus on helping them provide high-quality, cost-effective surgery.

American Association of Pediatric Plastic Surgeons (AAPPS)
500 Cummings Center, Suite 4550
Beverly, MA 01915
(978) 927-8330 • fax: (978) 524-8890
website: http://pediatricplasticsurgery.org

The American Association of Pediatric Plastic Surgeons is a membership organization focused on the specialties of pediatric plastic surgery and reconstructive plastic surgery for children with deformities. The organization's active members are board-certified pediatric plastic surgeons, but it also has an affiliate membership composed of medical residents, registered nurses, and research scientists who work in this field. The AAPPS was created in order to meet the need for discussion and development meetings among specialists in this field.

American Board of Cosmetic Surgery (ABCS)
8840 Calumet Ave., Suite 205
Munster, IN 46321
(219) 836-8585 • fax: (219) 836-5525
website: www.americanboardcosmeticsurgery.org

The American Board of Cosmetic Surgery sets requirements for the examination and certification of cosmetic surgeons in order to provide the public with a safe and ethical standard for the practice of cosmetic surgery. The organization was established in 1990 out of two existing cosmetic surgery boards and is structured around a board of trustees, independent officers, and an executive director. The ABCS maintains that the surgeons it certifies "shall demonstrate the highest standards of training, knowledge, and expertise, as determined by a process of peer review and standardized examination and certification."

American Board of Plastic Surgery (ABPS)
7 Penn Center, Suite 400
1635 Market Street
Philadelphia, PA 19103-2204
(215) 587-9322
e-mail: info@abplsurg.org
website: www.abplsurg.org

The American Board of Plastic Surgery is a nonprofit organization that seeks to protect the public by maintaining standards for the certification of physicians who specialize in plastic surgery. Founded in 1937, the board is one of twenty-four specialty boards that form the American Board of Medical Specialties. Physicians must meet specific educational, training, and professional requirements in order to achieve and maintain board certification as specialists in the field of plastic surgery through the ABPS. ABPS-certified plastic surgeons are listed in the *Official ABMS Directory of Board-Certified Medical Specialists*.

American Society of Cosmetic Breast Surgery (ASCBS)
1419 Superior Ave., Suite 2
Newport Beach, CA 92663
(949) 645-6665 • fax (949) 645-6784
e-mail: ascbsweb@yahoo.com
website: www.ascbs.org

The American Society of Cosmetic Breast Surgery was founded in 1985 by a group of surgeons specializing in breast implants and cosmetic breast surgery. The organization provides professionals with education and training and promotes the exchange of ideas and the advancement of research in this specialty. In the ASCBS annual meetings, ASCBS faculty surgeons provide expert training in surgical techniques to professionals in attendance, focusing on enhancing their surgery skills and knowledge. Through these activities the organization aims to improve "the opportunities of all women to eliminate deformities, have an attractive, normal chest, and improve the quality of their lives."

American Society of Ophthalmic Plastic and Reconstructive Surgery (ASOPRS)
5841 Cedar Lake Road, Suite 204
Minneapolis, MN 55416
(952) 646-2038 • fax: (952) 545-6073
website: www.asoprs.org

The American Society of Ophthalmic Plastic and Reconstructive Surgery was founded in 1969 to bring together surgeons specializing in cosmetic and reconstructive surgery of the face, eye sockets, eyelids, and tear-duct system. The organization's focus includes promoting education and research within this highly specialized field, as well as advancing the quality of clinical practice. Made up of more than 550 members from around the world, the ASOPRS provides specialized training to physicians and sponsors a variety of scientific meetings annually.

American Society of Plastic Surgeons (ASPS)
444 E. Algonquin Road
Arlington Heights, IL 60005
(847) 228-9900
website: www.plasticsurgery.org

With a membership of more than seven thousand physicians, the American Society of Plastic Surgeons is the largest plastic surgery organization of its kind worldwide. Founded in 1931, ASPS played a key role in the late 1930s in convincing the American Board of Surgery to establish an American Board of Plastic Surgery (ABPS). Until then plastic surgery had not been officially recognized as a unique discipline. ASPS states that its mission is "to advance quality care to plastic surgery patients by encouraging high standards of training, ethics, physician practice and research in plastic surgery." As part of the organization's advocacy of patient safety, ASPS physician members are held to strict requirements concerning their staff and facilities. The organization's website provides information to those interested in learning more about plastic surgery procedures or in selecting a qualified surgeon.

International Society of Aesthetic Plastic Surgery (ISAPS)
45 Lyme Road, Suite 304
Hanover, NH 03755
(603) 643-2325 • fax: (603) 643-1444

website: www.isaps.org

The International Society of Aesthetic Plastic Surgery is an international membership organization made up of more than twenty-four hundred reconstructive and aesthetic plastic surgeons from ninety-four countries. The organization was founded in 1970 in order to provide a forum for the exchange of ideas and knowledge in the field of cosmetic surgery internationally. Toward this end, it sponsors scientific meetings worldwide to keep its members abreast of the latest developments in technology and technique and publishes an academic journal titled *Aesthetic Plastic Surgery*. The organization's website provides the public with information on plastic surgery procedures and medical tourism as well as an international directory of ISAPS surgeons.

Society of Plastic Surgical Skin Care Specialists (SPSSCS)
11262 Monarch Street
Garden Grove, CA 92841
(562) 799-0466; toll-free: (800) 486-0611 • fax: (562) 799-1098
e-mail: info@spsscs.org
website: www.spsscs.org

The Society of Plastic Surgical Skin Care Specialists was formed in 1994 to address the need for an educational forum in the relatively new field of plastic surgical skin care. As a volunteer, nonprofit organization, it focuses on ensuring that safe and high-quality skin care is provided to patients in both the United States and Canada through education and skills training for professionals in this specialty. The SPSSCS is endorsed, or recognized, by the American Society for Aesthetic Plastic Surgery and the American Society of Plastic Surgeons.

For Further Reading

Books

Aston, Sherrel J., Douglas S. Steinbrech, and Jennifer L. Walden. *Aesthetic Plastic Surgery: Expert Consult.* Philadelphia: Saunders, 2012. An organized approach to the current techniques used in plastic surgery. The book includes DVDs and access to a website for a complete educational experience.

Davis, Kathy. *Reshaping the Female Body: The Dilemma of Cosmetic Surgery.* New York: Routledge, 2013. A medical sociologist tries to codify the complex decision-making process women undergo when deciding whether to alter their appearance surgically and to reconcile how a feminist could choose to alter her body to fit the "gendered social order" and remain a feminist.

Falcon, Dawn. *Breast Reduction Surgery Tips: What You Need to Know Before You Have Breast Reduction Surgery.* N.p.: Zacate Press, 2012. E-book. What can you expect during and after breast reduction surgery? This book will answer the majority of your questions regarding this procedure.

Flaharty, Patrick M. *Look Younger Now: Fillers, Face Lifts and Everything in Between—a 21st Century Guide.* Seattle: CreateSpace, 2012. If you are into antiaging in terms of what you see in the mirror, then this book is for you.

Harris-Moore, Deborah. *Media and the Rhetoric of Body Perfection: The Cultural Politics of Media and Popular Culture.* Burlington, VT: Ashgate, 2014. Drawing on rich interview material with cosmetic surgery patients and offering fresh analyses of various texts from popular culture, this book examines the ways in which Western media capitalize on body anxiety by presenting physical perfection as a moral imperative, while advertising quick and effective transformation methods to erase physical imperfections.

Janis, Jeffrey E. *Essentials of Plastic Surgery.* 2nd Ed. Boca Raton, FL: CRC, 2014. This book presents essential topics in aesthetic and reconstructive surgery. Coverage includes aesthetic surgery, face lift, neck lift, fillers, and breast augmentation, along with reconstructive topics such as wound healing and microsurgery.

Lin, Samuel J. *Aesthetic Head and Neck Surgery: McGraw-Hill Plastic Surgery Atlas.* New York: McGraw-Hill Professional, 2013. This is a full-color, step-by-step atlas of aesthetic head and neck surgery techniques.

Lycka, Barry. *Inside Cosmetic Surgery Today: In-Depth Conversations with the World's Leading Cosmetic Surgeons; Rejuvenating Hair as Women Age—Dr. Alan J. Bauman.* Amazon Digital Services, 2014. This book provides the latest information on minimally invasive hair transplants, low-level laser therapy, eyebrow and eyelash transplantation, as well as results-oriented hair-loss management procedures.

Northrop, Jane Megan. *Reflecting on Cosmetic Surgery: Body Image, Shame and Narcissism.* New York: Routledge, 2013. With a grounded approach, engaging thirty women through in-depth interviews, this study explores how they chose cosmetic surgery as an option.

Shiffman, Melvin A., and Alberto Di Giuseppe. *Cosmetic Surgery: Art and Techniques.* New York: Springer, 2012. This is an atlas of general cosmetic surgery that provides precise step-by-step descriptions of a full range of techniques, supported by photographs and illustrations.

Wen, Hua. *Buying Beauty: Cosmetic Surgery in China.* Hong Kong: Hong Kong University Press, 2013. Cosmetic surgery in China has grown rapidly in the recent years of dramatic social transition. Facing fierce competition in all spheres of daily life, more and more women consider cosmetic surgery an investment to gain "beauty capital" to increase opportunities for social and career success.

Williams, Edvin. *Rhinoplasty: Everything You Need to Know About Fixing and Reshaping Your Nose.* Seattle: CreateSpace, 2013. An internationally recognized board-certified facial plastic surgeon answers the most frequently asked questions about this common procedure.

Periodicals and Internet Sources

Asia Pacific Post. "Asian Eyes Are In as Beauty Ideals Shift," May 7, 2008.

Bernstein-Wax, Jessica. "Mexican Doctor Charged with Posing as Plastic Surgeon, Botching Dozens of Operations," Associated Press, December 28, 2007. www.ap.org.

Bilefsky, Dan. "If Plastic Surgery Won't Convince You, What Will?," *New York Times*, May 24, 2009.

Burton, Robert. "How Looks Can Kill," *Salon*, January 31, 2008. www.salon.com.

Charney, Ruth. "The Many Faces of Plastic Surgery," wowOwow, June 17, 2009. www.wowowow.com.

Cognard-Black, Jennifer. "Extreme Makeover: Feminist Edition," *Ms.*, Summer 2007.

Cohen, Elizabeth. "What Really Killed the Beauty Queen?," CNN, December 10, 2009. www.cnn.com.

Corrigan, Maura. "Stay Safe at the Med Spa," *Self*, August 2009.

Diller, Vivian. "Cosmetics Drugs Gone Too Far: Is Anything Still Real?," *Psychology Today*, July 14, 2010.

Flora, Carlin. "The Beguiling Truth About Beauty: Not a Knockout?," *Psychology Today*, May–June 2006.

Heelan, Charis Atlas. "Cosmetic Surgery Tourism: A Tummy Tuck in Thailand, a Breast Augmentation in Brazil," Frommers, September 6, 2005. www.frommers.com.

Kaufman, Dean. "Do You Think You're Beautiful?," *O, The Oprah Magazine*, April 2006.

Keane, Caomhan, and Leah Sullivan. "In Defense of Plastic Surgery," *The Dubliner*, February 19, 2008.

Lett, Dan. "The Search for Integrity in the Cosmetic Surgery Market," *Canadian Medical Association Journal*, January 29, 2008.

Medical News Today. "Cosmetic Surgery Patients at More Risk than Ever," November 16, 2009.

Payne, January W. "Autopsy of Kanye West's Mother Underscores Surgery Risks," *U.S. News & World Report*, January 17, 2008.

Phillips, Dominic. "Is Plastic Surgery Dangerous?," *Sunday Times* (London), December 13, 2009.

Shulman, Matthew. "Teens Getting Plastic Surgery: Be Cautious," *U.S. News & World Report*, July 1, 2008.

Smith, Rich. "Patient Satisfaction Is Key," Plastic Surgery Practice, January 2009. www.plasticsurgerypractice.com.

Swain, Andrew D. "The Hidden Dangers of 'Medical' Spas," *Trial*, May 1, 2009.

Websites

The Cosmetic Surgery Directory Blog (http://cosmeticsurgeryblog .the-cosmetic-surgery-directory.com). This directory/blog is a valuable resource for individuals seeking a board-certified cosmetic or plastic surgeon. In addition the blog is a central resource that answers questions about plastic surgery and shares unusual news and perspectives on plastic surgeries.

Plastic Surgery Post (www.plasticsurgery.org/news/plastic-surgery -blog.html). The American Society of Plastic Surgeons' blog provides a great resource for consumers to learn about members who are qualified to perform surgery.

RealSelf: Reviews of Cosmetic Treatments, Surgery, Doctors (www.realself.com). Featured on this site are consumer reviews of more than 250 cosmetic treatments. In addition, the site helps consumers choose from more than twelve thousand board-certified doctors and receive personalized answers from medical experts.

Truth in Cosmetic Surgery (www.cosmeticsurgerytruth.com/blog). This blog is designed to entertain as well as educate the potential plastic surgery patient. The author, John Di Saia (aka Dr. D), points to obvious scams, answers reader questions, and does "celebrity surgery analysis" for entertainment.

Index

Eyebrow transplants, 60*t*
Eyelid surgery. *See* Blepharoplasty

F
Face-lifts
availability, 7
botched surgery case study,
38–39
favoring of, by women, 61
mid-60s men, 110–111
popularity, 64
risk factors, 13, 15
senior citizens, 94
social media data, 60*t*
Facial deformities, 88
Facial implants, 60*t*
Familial bonding, 61
Farrior, Edward, 8, 58–59, 62
Fat freezing, 21
Faunch, Cheryl, 38–39
Feminist viewpoint of cosmetic
surgery, 76–79
Fonda, Jane, 102
Food and Drug Administration
(FDA)
breast implant follow-up
guidelines, 34
breast implant risks, 24
device approval as lax, 21
fat freezing approval, 21
low-level laser light approval,
19
teen breast augmentation rule,
85
Foot binding, cosmetic surgery
comparison, 64
Forbes, Lynn, 66–67

Ford, Betty, 102
Forehead lift, 60*t*, 95
Foreign cosmetic surgery. *See*
Medical tourism

G
Ganahl, Jane, 63–69
Germany, 52
Goudreau, Jenna, 11–16
Graham, Mary, 95
Great Plastic Surgery Debate, six
lessons
avoidance of present moment,
65–66
being judged/judging others,
67
dealing with impermanence,
66
embracing of authentic self,
68
invisibility of older women,
66–67
researching potential risks,
67–68
Green, Laura, 41–42

H
Hair transplants
AAFPRS survey data, 58
male popularity, 61
social media data, 60*t*
Hansen, Juliana, 29–35
Harvard Medical School, 97
Hughes, James, 96
Hullett, Joseph, 14–15
Human "Ken" doll, *43*
Hyaluronic acid injections, *53*,
61, *90*

Men (*continued*)
  breast reduction, *90*
  face-lifts, 110–111
  hair transplant popularity, 61
  minimally invasive proce-
    dures, *107*
  Phillips, Colin, suicide, 47
  reasons for surgery, 7–8
  senior citizens, 95
  types of surgery requests, 59
Mercer, Nigel, 50
Meyer, Gilbert, 95
Mothers as patients, *77*
Motivations for pursuing cosmetic surgery, 49, 72–75
MRI (magnetic resonance imaging), 32–33

N
Nagelin-Anderson, Elizabeth, 24
Naish, John, 44–50
National Health Service (NHS),
  39, 41, 49
Nduka, Charles, 49–50
Neck liposuction, 59
Neustatter, Angela, 76–79
Niccole, Michael, 96
Noninvasive skin tightening, 19,
  21
Nonsurgical procedures
  AAFPRS survey, 59
  Botox, 61
  patients sixty-five and over,
    94*t*
  risk factors, 85
  teen procedures, *90*
  2013, patient ratings, *53*
  2013, procedure totals, *65*

2013, US spending data, *12*
  women, percentages, 61
Northwestern Medicine study,
  18
Nose job. *See* Rhinoplasty

O
O'Brien, Elizabeth, 106–111
Olson, Hannah, 82, 84–85
Otoplasty (ears), 60*t*

P
Parents
  negative self-esteem promo-
    tion, 73–74
  risk factor awareness, 8, 15,
    85
  Sophy, Charles, advice, 82–
    83
Patient ratings, top procedures
  (2013), *53*
Paul, Marla, 17–22
Peels/microdermabrasion, *53*,
  61, 94*t*, *107*, 108
Pellot, Emerald, 7
People (magazine), 84
Phillips, Colin, 47
Pietras, Emma, 36–42
Pillarella, Laura, 44–46, 48
Plastic and Reconstructive Surgery
  (journal), 46, 95
Post-surgical reactions, 8–9
Poupard, Richard J., 70–75
Present Shock (Rushkoff), 66
Pretty Hurts (Beyoncé), 91
Pros and cons of cosmetic sur-
  gery, 8–9
Psychological counseling, 49

Picture Credits

© Alex Bartel/Science Source, 100
© AlexSutula/Shutterstock.com, 73
© allOver images/Alamy, 10
© Amanda Edwards/Getty Images, 43
© Ariwasabi/Shutterstock.com, 54
© Biophoto Associates/Science Source, 30
© BSIP SA/Alamy, 84
© Eight Arts Photography/Alamy, 19
© leungchopan/Shutterstock.com, 58
© Monkey Business Images/Shutterstock.com, 93, 109
© moodboard/Alamy, 14
© Patrick T. Fallon/Bloomberg via Getty Images, 80
© Vladimir Gjorgiev/Shutterstock.com, 48
© Voisin/Phanie/Science Source, 25
© Woohae Cho/Bloomberg via Getty Images, 40

Russell Memorial Library
88 Main Street
Acushnet, MA 02743

ACUSHNET   YANFIC
32032005021576
Y 617.952 COS
Greenhaven Press
Cosmetic Surgery

DISCARD

7/15